Italian Academy Training Sessions for U15 - U19

A Complete Soccer Coaching Program from the Italian Serie

Written By the
Soccer Italian Style Coaches

Mirko Mazzantini

Simone Bombardieri

Published By

Italian Academy Training Sessions for U15 - U19

A Complete Soccer Coaching Program from the Italian Serie 'A'

First Published September 2011 by SoccerTutor.com
This Edition Published May 2012 by SoccerTutor.com

Info@soccertutor.com I www.SoccerTutor.com
UK: 0208 1234 007 I **US**: (305) 767 4443 I **ROTW**: +44 208 1234 007

ISBN 978-0-9566752-2-4

Authors
Soccer Italian Style (Mirko Mazzantini and Simone Bombardieri) © 2011

Edited by
Richard Bond

Cover and book design by
Alex Macrides, Think Out Of The Box Ltd.
email: design@thinkootb.com Tel: +44 (0) 208 144 3550

Diagrams
Diagram designs by SoccerTutor.com. All the diagrams in this book have been created using SoccerTutor.com Tactics Manager Software available from
www.SoccerTutor.com

Note: While every effort has been made to ensure the technical accuracy of the content of this book, neither the author nor publishers can accept any responsibility for any injury or loss sustained as a result of the use of this material.

Meet the Coaches of Soccer Italian Style

Mirko Mazzantini
"ACF Fiorentina Academy Coach"

Mirko Mazzantini coached for Empoli FC for 10 years, at almost all the main age groups of the academy level. In 2010 he was then recruited by AFC Fiorentina working with the U14/U15 Academy teams. During the 2010/11 season Mirko won the U15 Italian Academy Serie 'A' championship. UEFA 'B' Coach and author of many coaching publications, articles, books and DVDs.

Simone Bombardieri
"Empoli FC Academy Coach"

Simone Bombardieri played as a player in the Empoli FC club for 5 years. He then started his career as a coach being recruited by Empoli FC where he has been coaching the academy age groups in the last 9 years from U9 – U14. This coming season Simone is in charge of the U15 Academy team. UEFA 'B' Coach and author of many coaching publications, articles, books and DVDs.

Introduction

Contents

Session 11

Session 12

Soccer Italian Style Philosophy

Soccer Italian Style was born in 2005. Mirko Mazzantini (ACF Fiorentina) and Simone Bombardieri (Empoli FC) are both professional academy coaches of the Italian Serie 'A'. They have combined due to their great passion for youth development and they have embarked on a joint project that has taken them to various other parts of the world such as the United States, Canada, France and Norway.

The Soccer Italian style philosophy is made up of the principal features of the Italian style series and Mirko and Simone's vast experiences of professional training in Italy and football worldwide. The book outlines a training methodology that is simple and efficient which the authors have personally tested over time throughout their careers in Italy. **They have been highly successful in producing top players who are both technically and tactically astute.**

The success of this program has been demonstrated by the numerous academy victories against the main teams in Italy and European football with far greater resources. Mirko's Under 15 team at Fiorentina won the Italian Academy League in 2010-11 beating teams such as AC MIlan, Inter Milan and Juventus to the title.

Many players who have been trained using this exact program in Italy have gone on to professional careers and have been capped for the Italian national teams in various age groups, where before this was simply not the case.

This book contains 12 training sessions with each session focused on fundamental technical or tactical coaching that is analysed throughout the 6 practices. The 12 sessions have been developed to demonstrate the need of progressions in training, using the basic principle **"from simple to complex"**.

Inside the two volumes there are general team exercises that are useful for all coaches and players in every position, but there are also many specific exercises that are designated for individual roles or positions within a team (e.g. attackers, midfielders or defenders).

Mirko and Simone have a high expertise in technical training and they have developed activities that are open to numerous variations which means that the 12 sessions can be used over and over to make this program of training even more complete.

This passion has driven the pair to "write on paper" what they have learned and experienced up to today, with a great hope that this method will be greatly enjoyed by the readers and used throughout the world to create top quality professional players.

Soccer Italian Style
Mirko Mazzantini & Simone Bombardieri

Session Format

There are at least 6 practices in each of the 12 sessions with some having additional progressions.

All 12 sessions always start with:
Practice 1 - Warm-up always with the ball
Practice 2 - Football specific conditioning
Practice 3 - 6 cover both technical and tactical practices.

Each practice includes clear diagrams with supporting training notes such as:
- Name of Practice
- Objective of Practice
- Coaching Points of Practice
- Variations or Progression of Practice (if applicable)
- Coaching Points of Practice.

Key

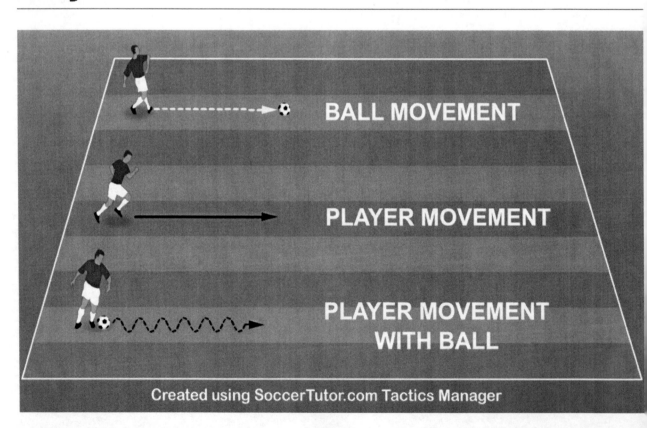

Session 1

Technical Warm-Up - Ball Control

20 Minutes

Created using SoccerTutor.com Tactics Manager

Objective

To develop ball control in a technical warm-up.

Description

The team is divided into two groups.

The first group juggles the ball individually, changing the theme every minute (right foot only, right left only, one left-one right, two left-two right, inside left-inside right, 4 touches by feet and one by head etc).

At the same time, the second group juggles in pairs. The first player, after passing the ball to his teammate, performs a coordination action such as a forward roll, a backwards roll, five high knees to chest, five alternate side-volley kicks or five lateral movements to the right and left. The second player will juggle, pass the ball and will also perform a coordination action. As soon as the first player finishes, he should be ready to receive the ball.

Every minute the coach will change the coordination Practice. After 10 minutes the groups will change.

Stretch after 5, 10, 15 and 20 minutes

Coaching Points

1. Individual: Soft feel and touch of the ball
2. Pairs: Be on the balls of your feet

20 Minutes

Football Specific Conditioning

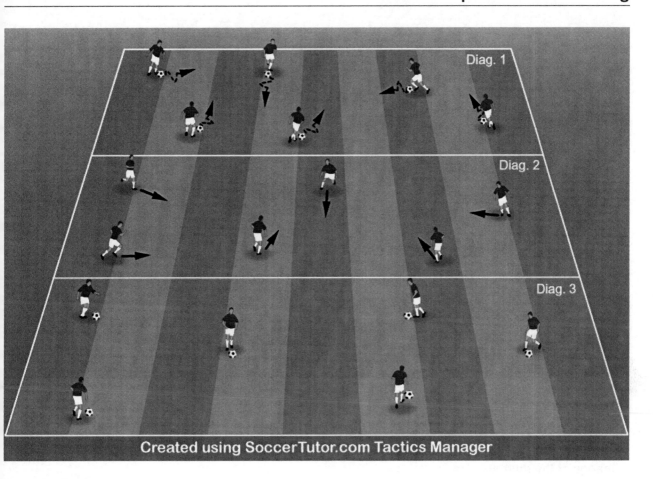

Diag. 1

Diag. 2

Diag. 3

Created using SoccerTutor.com Tactics Manager

Objective

To build the athletic bases for football-specific movements (endurance aerobic drills).

Description

10 minutes: Free running in the space with the ball (intensity level: 80%). **Diagram 1**

5 minutes: Stretching

5 minutes: Interval Training - (running with speed variation) 50 seconds slow – 10 seconds fast. **Diagram 2**

2 minutes: Active recovery, running slow with the ball in the space. **Diagram 3**

Technical Work - Dribbling and Coordination

15 Minutes

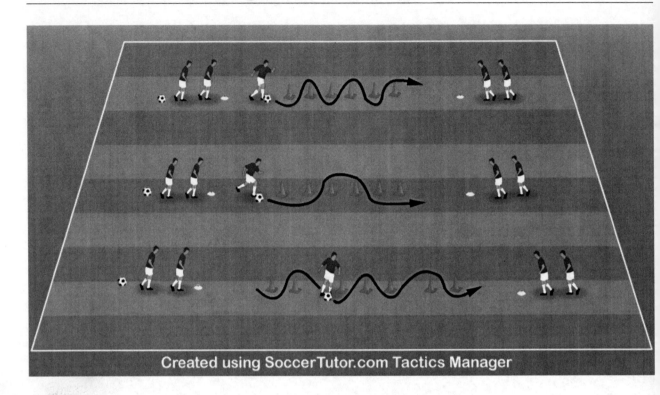

Created using SoccerTutor.com Tactics Manager

Objective

To develop coordination and a change of the rhythm when players are dribbling with the ball.

Description

Change of the rhythm:

All the team is divided in 3 lines;

1. In the first line, players must dribble in and out the cones one by one.

2. In the second line, players dribble in and out every two by two cones.

3. In the third line, players dribble in and out the cones one by one, but notice the distances of the cones will change the rhythm compared to the first line.

Coaching Points:

1. It is necessary to have a good control of the ball (soft touch at speed) with the aim of dribbling through all of the cones without errors.
2. Slightly bent knees, keeping the ball near the feet
3. Make many touches with the ball
4. Soft feel with the ball

15 Minutes

Individual Attacking and Defending Practices

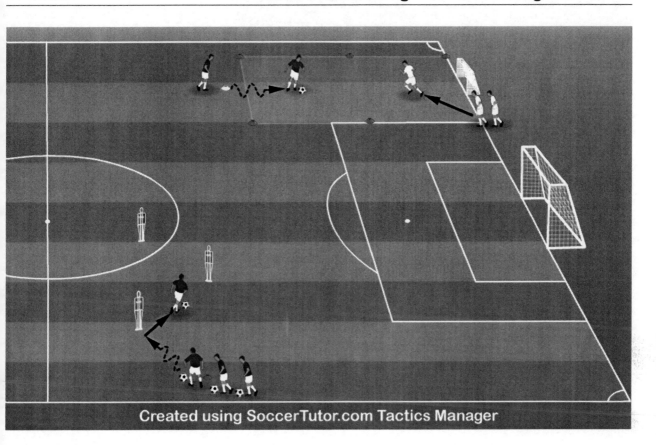

Created using SoccerTutor.com Tactics Manager

Objective
To develop marking "The Italian Way" and improve attacking moves/feints.

Description
The team is divided into two groups:

The first group:
1v1 Scenario.
The defender passes to the forward and on his first touch must defend; closing the space down. The forward must try to score in the small goal. The defenders objective is to protect the goal and force the ball out of play.

The second group (forwards and midfielders)
Players start by dribbling towards the first mannequin (use a traffic cone if you haven't got mannequins) and then make a move, feint or fake (i.e. Scissors move) and accelerate away to the 2nd mannequin. Use the same move for all three mannequins for 2 minutes then change the move.

Individual Attacking and Defending Practices

Coaching Points

(Defenders):

The focus is marking in a frontal situation so the most important aspects are:

1. Assess the opponent's speed
2. Running speed of the defender, slowing down before approaching
3. Position of both feet of the defender (always with a foot in front, never with both feet in the same line). This is also known as the 'Jockey' or 'Surfer' position.
4. The defender must direct the forward onto his weaker foot

(Forwards & Midfielders):

1. Keep ball close to the feet
2. Exaggerate the move/feint
3. Change of the speed after feinting past the mannequins

15 Minutes

Game Situations - Marking Ability

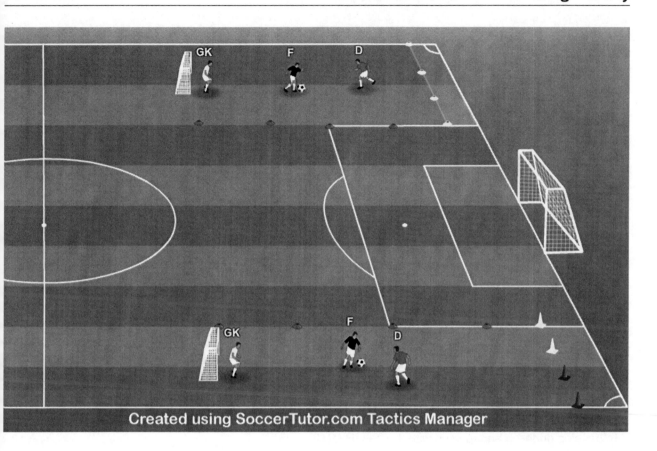

Created using SoccerTutor.com Tactics Manager

Objective
To improve marking marking ability in a game situations.

Description
Game 1: "1 v 1 End Zone"
The game starts with the defender passing the ball to the forward who, on his first touch, must defend; being sure to close the space down. The forward earns one point if stops the ball in the end-zone. If the defender wins the ball, he can shoot on goal but he has only 3 seconds in which to do so.

Game 2: "1 v 1 Target Goals"
The game starts with the defender passing the ball to the forward who, on his first touch, must defend; being sure to close the space down. The forward earns one point if he successfully dribbles through one of the small coned goals (blue and yellow). If the defender wins the ball, he can shoot on goal but he has only 3 seconds in which to do so.

Coaching Points
1. Assess the opponent's speed
2. Try to force the opponent onto his weaker side

Small Sided Game - Dribbling and RWTB

15 Minutes

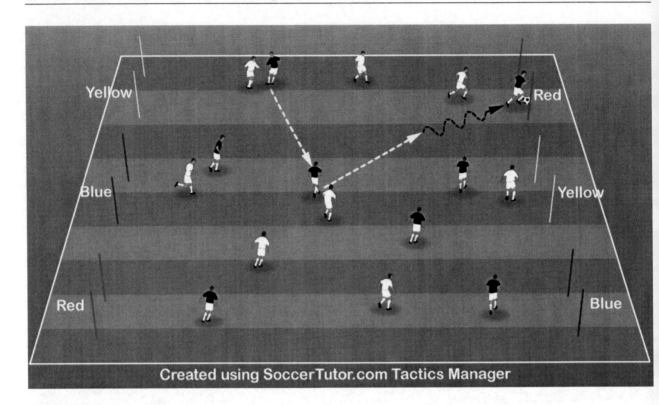

Created using SoccerTutor.com Tactics Manager

Objective
To develop dribbling and running with the ball (RWTB).

Description
In a field area of 40 x 30 yards, there are 6 goals (two red, two yellow and two blue).

The objective is to score in any of the goals by dribbling/running with the ball through the goal and then stopping it.

For the first 8 minutes, players can enter in all the goals. In the final 8 minutes, the coach will call out the colour where both teams can enter, changing it every time he deems appropriate.

Coaching Points
1. Play and think quickly
2. Create space, losing your marker to receive the pass
3. Try to do a different feint/move every time to get away from your marker

Session 2

Warm-Up - Two Small Sided Games

20 Minutes

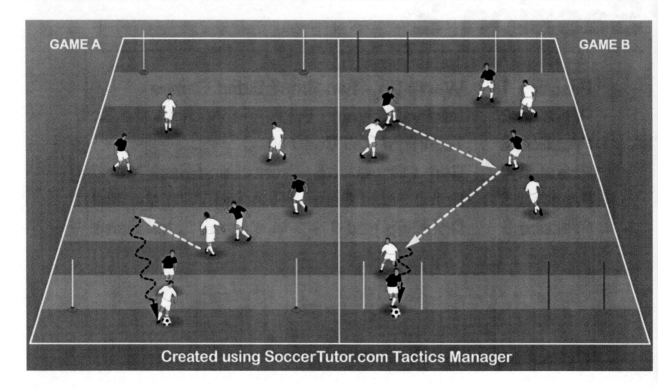

Created using SoccerTutor.com Tactics Manager

Objective

To develop the dribbling and running with the ball in small sided games.

Description

The team is divided into two groups. There are two different games.

Game A: "Rugby Game"

The objective is to run with the ball between the boundary poles and score a point by stopping the ball with sole of the foot. Players can only dribble/run with the ball and pass backwards, just like in rugby.

Game B: "4 Goals Match"

This game's objective is to dribble/run with the ball through the goals (between the boundary poles) before stopping the ball within the area. A good variant could be if the coach changes the "objective" by calling out a respective colour during the match.

Stretch after 5, 10, 15 and 20 minutes

Coaching Points

1. Play and think quickly
2. Try to do a different feint/move every time

Interval Training With and Without the Ball

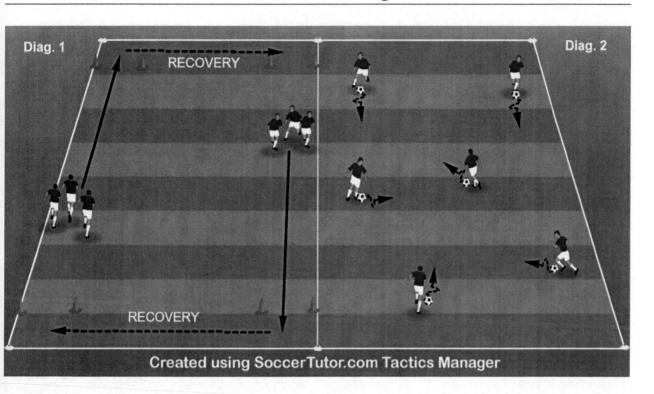

Diag. 1

RECOVERY

RECOVERY

Diag. 2

Created using SoccerTutor.com Tactics Manager

Objective

To build the athletic bases for football using interval training.

Description

The team is divided into two groups, which work simultaneously until they change.

5 minutes: 6 repetitions 200 meters (max speed – slow jog recovery before restarting).

You can also introduce a ball to each player. *Diagram 1*

5 minutes: Stretching

10 minutes: Running with the ball (1 minute slow – 1 minute fast) *Diagram 2*

2 minutes: Recovery rest before moving on to the next stage of the session.

Technical Ball Control

15 Minutes

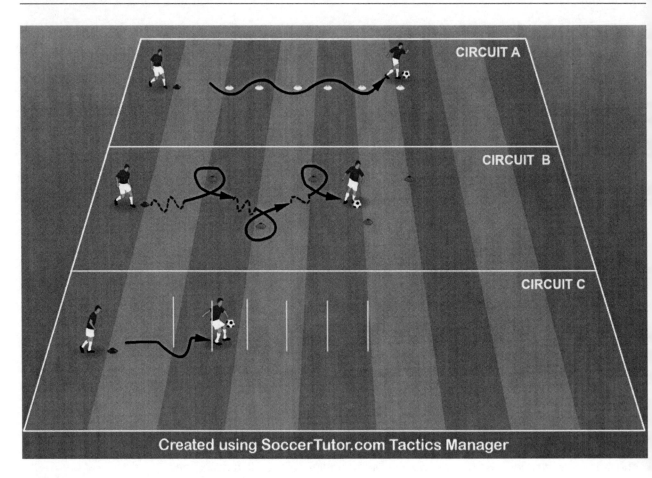

CIRCUIT A

CIRCUIT B

CIRCUIT C

Created using SoccerTutor.com Tactics Manager

Objective
Three different circuits to improve dribbling and control.

Description
CIRCUIT A:
Players dribble in and out of all the cones (distance 50 cm) and then pass the ball to the next player in line.

Variants:
- Right foot only,
- Left foot only,
- Switching both feet,
- Outside left and right,
- Inside-outside left and right.

Technical Ball Control

CIRCUIT B:
Players dribble around the cones in a diagonal eight figure pattern.
Players then pass the ball to the next player in line.

Variants:
- Right foot only,
- Left foot only,
- Inside feet,
- Outside feet.

Try to do it with many and fast touches.

CIRCUIT C:
Players must juggle the ball inside and outside of the boundary poles.
Players then pass the ball to the next player in line.

Variants:
- Right foot only,
- Left foot only,
- Both feet
- One touch left one touch right,
- Both thigh,
- Two by feet, two thighs.

Coaching Points
1. Make many touches with the ball
2. Soft feel with the ball

Game Situations - Frontal and Back Marking
15 Minutes

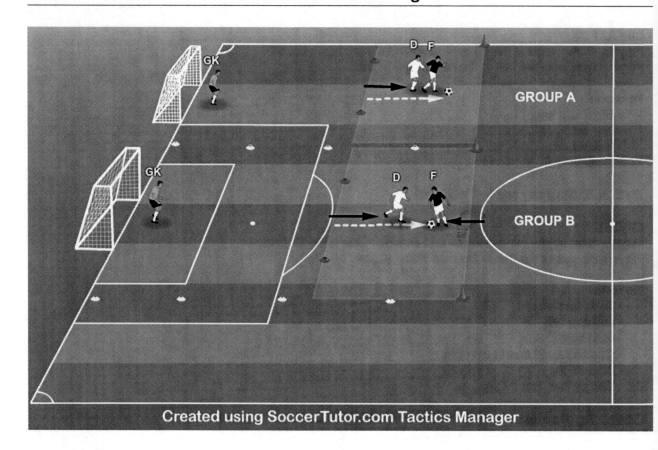

GROUP A

GROUP B

Created using SoccerTutor.com Tactics Manager

Objective
Game situations to improve the marking ability (frontal and back marking).

Description
GROUP A: "Back marking"
Both the defender and forward start between the red disc-cones. The defender passes the ball in front of the forward, who in turn must try to turn, advance beyond the red disc-cones and shoot on goal. The defender must try to prevent the forward from turning. The right distance for the defender is approximately 50cm. This distance permits to intervene in an easy way when the forward tries to turn.

GROUP B: "Frontal marking"
The defender passes the ball to the forward in front of him, after receiving the ball he must try to enter the end zone, which is beyond the red disc-cones, and shoot on goal. The defender must try to prevent the forward from entering the end zone and force the ball out of play.

The coach will change both groups after 7 minutes.

Coaching Points
1. Asses the opponent's speed and try to force the opponent on his weaker side
2. Body shape – Be side on, known as the jockey/surfer position

15 Minutes   **Small Sided Game - Running With the Ball**

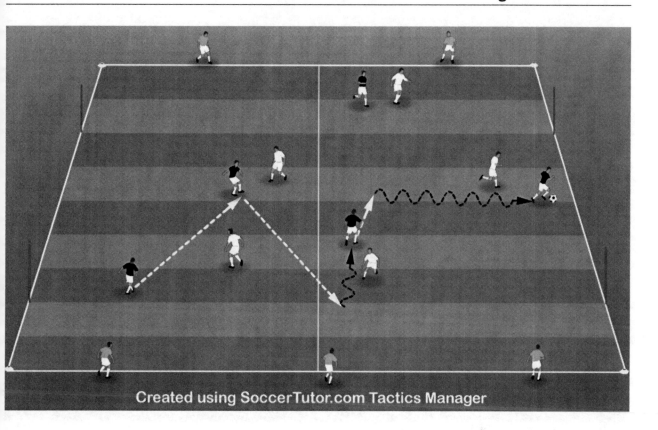

Created using SoccerTutor.com Tactics Manager

Objective
To develop running with the ball (RWTB)

Description
The teams are divided into 3 groups.
The red and blue teams play 5v5 in the middle. The yellow team waits out of the field.

When a team a scores (as shown in the diagram) by running with the ball through the boundary poles (can use cones) the opponent team comes out and the yellow team on the outside comes in.

Every time a team scores, they maintain possession and attack in the opposite direction.

There are two game conditions to consider:
1.   Players on the outside can be used but only have one touch
2.   First team to score 2 goals before changing the losing team

Coaching Points
1.   Play and think quickly
2.   Analyse the change of the game situation immediately
3.   Encourage to beat the opponent using different moves/feints

Dribbling and 1 v 1 in a Small Sided Game

20 Minutes

Created using SoccerTutor.com Tactics Manager

Objective

To develop dribbling and 1 v 1 with the GK in a small sided game.

Description

Up to 8v8 with two goalkeepers added.

The teams play in the central zone. The objective is to play a through ball or dribble outside the central zone for a 1 v 1 with the goalkeeper without opponents. In this case, the player must dribble and beat the goalkeeper before scoring.

If the team scores, they regain possession from their own goalkeeper. If a team fails to score then the opposition gains possession of the ball starting from their goalkeeper.

Coaching Points

1. In the central zone - create space for the opportunity to advance outside.
2. Attack directly at the goalkeeper. This makes it harder for the GK and gives the attacker option to go left or right.
3. Goalkeepers have the advantage of diving at the attackers feet so make the move/feint quickly and be decisive.

Session 3

Practice 1	Warm-Up - Dribbling and RWTB in a SSG
Practice 2	Speed, Power, Reaction and Acceleration
Practice 3	Technical Work - Ball Control, Feints & Dribbling
Practice 4	Real Game Situations - 1 v 1s and 2 v 2s
Practice 5	Man to Man Marking in a Small Sided Game
Practice 6	Free Small Sided Game - Half-Field

Warm-Up - Dribbling and RWTB in a SSG

15 Minutes

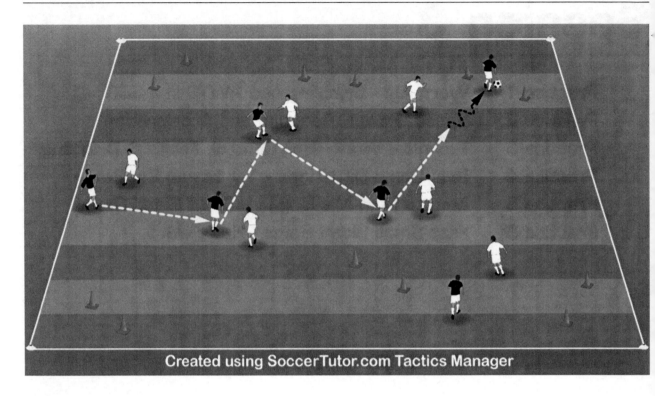

Created using SoccerTutor.com Tactics Manager

Objective

To develop the dribbling and running with the ball in a small sided game (SSG).

Description

Six goals (2 yards apart) are positioned randomly within the area. The objective is to run with the ball/dribble through the goals. When scored, maintain possession and look to score in another goal.

Stretch after 5, 10, and 15 minutes

Coaching Points

1. All players must always be moving, no walking for the duration of the warm-up.
2. Encourage receiving passes half-turned. This enables players to develop their awareness, which allows for quicker and better decision-making.
3. Encourage players to look up ahead so they can see the ball, players and the goals.

20 Minutes

Speed, Power, Reaction and Acceleration

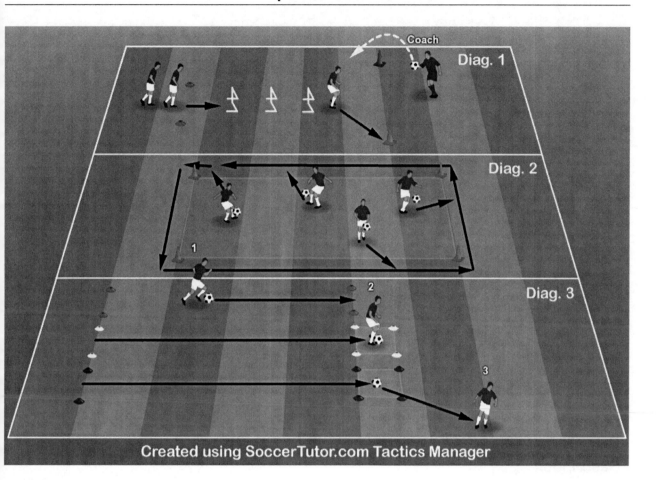

Created using SoccerTutor.com Tactics Manager

Objective
To develop players' speed, power, reaction times and acceleration both with and without the ball.

Description
The team is divided into three groups which work simultaneously until they change.

5 minutes: *Diagram 1:*
Player skips over the three hurdles, heads the ball back to the coach and sprints to the cone that is called out.

5 minutes: *Diagram 2:*
Players juggle the ball inside the area. Every 30 seconds the players will leave their ball and run around the area at maximum speed for 30 seconds.

5 minutes: *Diagram 3:*
Player 1 leans forward then sprints with the ball 20 yards.
Player 2 leans forward then sprints with the ball 20 yards before stopping inside the marked zone.
Player 3 does the same as player 2 but then changes direction for 5 yards.

10 repetitions for each of the three exercises.

Technical Work - Ball Control, Feints & Dribbling

10 Minutes

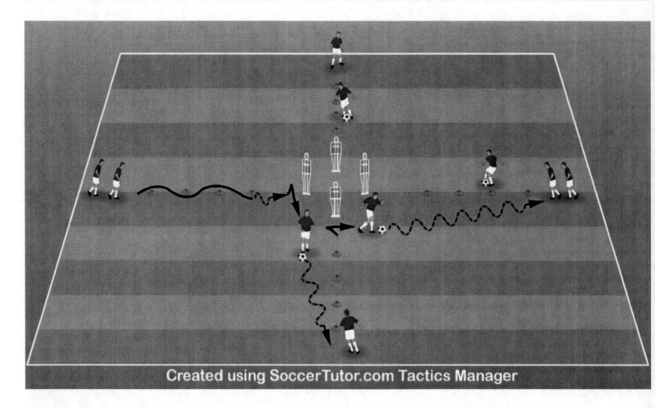

Created using SoccerTutor.com Tactics Manager

Objective

To develop ball control, feints and dribbling.

Description

This set up is called "The Star". You can set up one or more stations depending on how many players you have.

Four players start at the same time from all four sides of the star; they dribble in and out all the cones. As they approach the mannequin the players execute a move/feint then take the ball to the right and change their side.

Every 2 minutes the coach will change:
- The dribble sequence - i.e. dribble in and out every 2 cones etc.
- Technique - inside feet only, outside feet only etc.
- Type of move/feint
- Change the direction from anti-clockwise to clockwise

Coaching Points

1. Keep the ball close to the feet
2. Make many touches with the ball
3. Soft feel with the ball
4. Move/feint - exaggerate the move to faking to go one and go the other

Created using SoccerTutor.com Tactics Manager

Objective

To reproduce real game situations where running with the ball, dribbling and beating opponents are the most important aspects.

Description

Central zone of the field:

Two central defenders (blues), play against two midfielders/ forwards (reds) in a 2 v 2 duel. The game situation starts with one of the central midfielders passing to one of the midfielders/forwards to simulate a real match situation. The midfielders/forwards objective is to beat the defenders and advance past 18 yard line where either one of them can shoot on goal without opponents. If the central defenders win the ball then they can score a point by passing to one of the midfielders/forwards next in line.

Right and Left flank zones:

The full back ("defender") plays against the wide midfielder (also known as a "winger"). The game situation starts with the full back passing to the winger whose objective is to beat the defender and advance past 18 yard line, go around the boundary pole and deliver a "cross". The goalkeeper will try to take the ball training this particular game situation. The coach could ask to the winger to whip a cross to the near post or a deeper cross to the far post.

Real Game Situations - 1 v 1s and 2 v 2s

Objective

The diagram shows all three groups working at the same time however the coach can start off with only one group working at any given time then progress to all three groups working simultaneously.

This exercise will be particularly good for the goalkeeper's awareness having to potentially deal with 3 balls.

If you have two goalkeepers, then both can be working at the same time.

Coaching Points

(Defenders)

1. Assess the opponent's speed
2. Running speed of the defender, slowing down before approaching
3. Position of both feet of the defender (always with a foot in front, never with both feet in the same line). Also known as the 'Jockey' or 'Surfer' position.
4. The full back defenders must shape their opponents outside, close the flanks.
5. The central defenders must shape their opponent on their weaker side.

(Forwards & Midfielder's)

Flank Zones:

1. Keep ball close to the feet
2. Use a move/feint to beat your opponent
3. Before approaching the boundary pole, look up to assess the crossing options

Central Zone:

1. Create space to receive the bail in space
2. Mix up the attacking options making runs short, long, receiving to feet and also in behind the defenders
3. Encourage your players to take the opportunity to beat the defender and advance past the 18 yard line.
4. Encourage your players to express themselves, taking opportunities that they see.

Man to Man Marking in a Small Sided Game

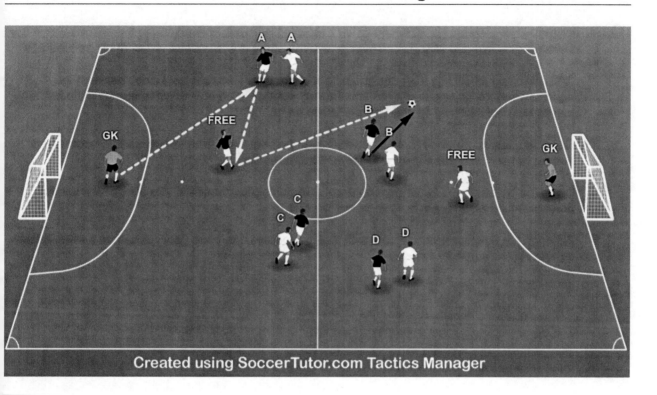

Created using SoccerTutor.com Tactics Manager

Objective

To develop man to man marking in a small sided game.

Description

In a reduced field, there are two teams of 5 players in addition to a goalkeeper.

Within each team there will be:
- One free player, without man to man marking, that cannot shot on goal
- Four players with a fixed man to man marking

Every player can only intervene on his particular opponent. The player who wins the duel can shoot on goal without pressure from other opponents, except for the "free player".

If a player loses his opponent who in turn strikes on goal, he must do 10 pushups. In this special man to man marking match, the coach can reproduce many game situations. Examples of these could be a central defender against a forward, left defender against right wing etc.

Man to Man Marking in a Small Sided Game

Coaching Points

1. Defenders should pay attention on the specific opponent, try to understand all of his peculiarities

2. Defenders should stick to their designated opponents and maintain 'goal side'; between the opponent and the goal, probably on a half-tuned position to be able to move quickly if the ball is played past the defender for the attacker to run on to.

3. Defenders should be close to their opponents, to prevent them from turning as they receive the ball but not so close that it is easy to play the ball in behind.

4. When the ball is played to the opponent, can the defender intercept it? Challenge it? If not the defender should not dive in but just jockey the ball.

5. Although the defenders should stick with their opponents, there are going to be times when a goal threatens. The defender may have to challenge another player.

15 Minutes

Free Small Sided Game - Half-Field

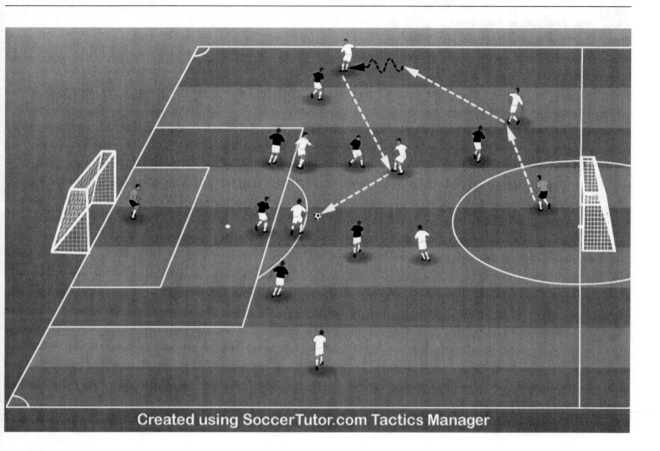

Created using SoccerTutor.com Tactics Manager

Objective
To take what the players learnt in the previous practice (Practice 5 of 6) in an unconditional game.

Description
On half a pitch set up 8 v 8 including goalkeepers in a free unconditional game.

Make sure that the players play in the positions that they played in during the previous practice (Practice 5 of 6); this way you can analyse their progress.

As you can see in the diagram, the blue team is set up with 4 defenders, 2 central midfielders and 1 forward. The red team is set up with 1 defender, 4 midfielders and 2 forwards.

Coaching Points
No coaching points. Just let the players play and express themselves.

Session 4

10 Minutes

Warm-Up - Possession in a Small Sided Game

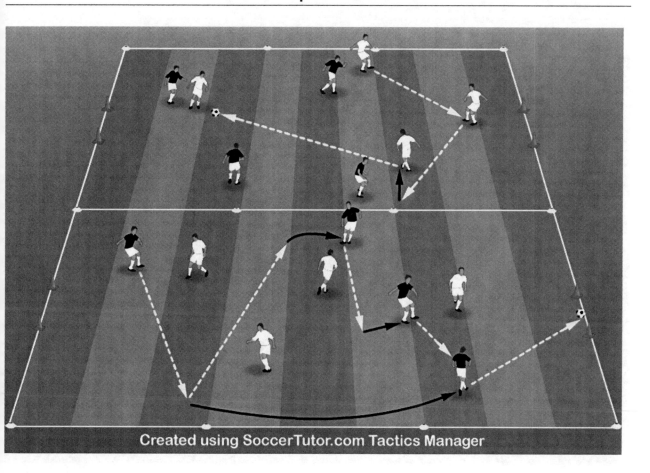

Created using SoccerTutor.com Tactics Manager

Objective
To develop possession of the ball in a small sided game.

Description
Two games, (5 v 5 or 4 v 4) are played simultaneously on a mini-field of 20 x 30 yards or 20 x 15 yards. The objective is possession of the ball. Each team can only score after making 4 consecutive passes. A variant could be:

- 2-touch – Maximum of 2 touches only
- Below knee height only - All the passes on the ground (below knee height), if the ball is goes in the air, possession of the ball changes to the opposite team

Stretch after 5 and 15 minutes

Coaching Points
1. Create space to find the right position on the field to receive the ball
2. Body shape and angle of support to receive and identify the next pass
3. Ask to play fast using only 2 touches when is possible
4. Reduce timing between the first touch (the receiving) and the second (passing)

Endurance Aerobic Conditioning

20 Minutes

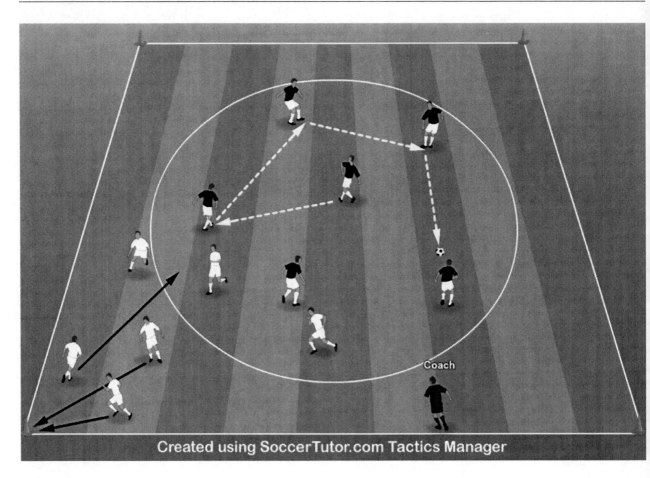

Created using SoccerTutor.com Tactics Manager

Objective
To build the athletic bases for football specific endurance aerobic conditioning.

Description
There are two teams inside the circle.

At the coach's command, the red team's players run out of the circle towards the cone of the coach's choice (i.e. by colour, number) and return back into the circle.

In the meantime, the blue team must pass the ball inside the circle as many times as possible, before all of the red players return.

Once the red team is back, the blue team runs out and the process is repeated.

There should be four repetitions of 2 minutes with a recovery time of 1 and a half minutes.

20 Minutes

Technical - Receiving the Ball in Space

Objective

To improve receiving the ball in space.

Description

The team is divided into 2 main groups:

GROUP 1 (Right Side):

Player 'A' starts in the middle of the surrounding boundary poles. The 'Server' passes the ball between the central red poles and calls out one of a possible 3 options. Player 'A' must receive the ball with the first touch, between one of three small gates. The 3 options, which gate player 'A' has to take the ball between, are:

1. Server calls **"CLOSE"** = Player 'A' receives the ball with the **INSIDE - RIGHT** of the foot taking it between **GATE 1** (the yellow and red pole)

2. Server calls **"OPEN"** = Player 'A' receives the ball with the **INSIDE - RIGHT** of the foot taking it between **GATE 2** (the red and blue pole)

3. Server calls **"OUTSIDE"** = Player 'A' receives the ball with the **OUTSIDE - RIGHT** of the foot taking it between **GATE 3** (the blue and yellow pole)

Technical - Receiving the Ball in Space

GROUP 2 (Left side):

Two central defenders (CB1 and CB2) start on the same centre cone. Player 'A' lofts the ball, at the same time CB1 and CB1 moves/sprints backwards to receive the pass (this simulation is a common defender situation) in the space and one of them makes the decision control it (CB1) in the opposite direction to CB2 who makes a run to either cone 1 or 2. CB1 then plays the ball back to player 'A'.

Variations (See Diagram below):

1. Receiving the ball with chest then passing it back to player 'A'

2. Receiving the ball with inside or outside volley foot, playing it directly to the partnering central defender who then passes back to player 'A'

3. Receiving the ball by head, playing it directly to the partnering central defender who then passes back to player 'A'

15 Minutes | **Tactical Player Positioning and Ball Recovery**

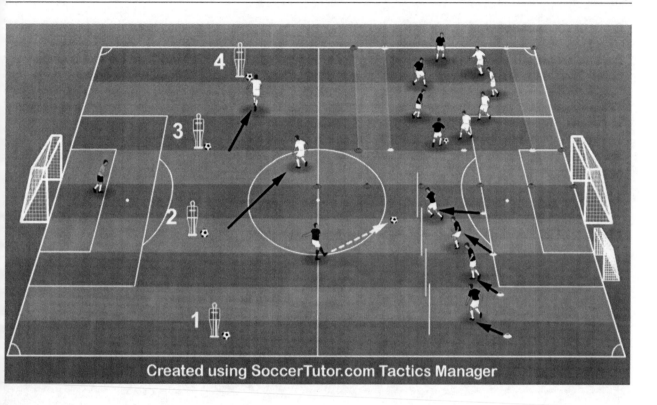

Created using SoccerTutor.com Tactics Manager

Objective
To develop a good team tactics with correct player positioning without the ball and attacking after ball recovery (system of play 4-4-2).

Description
GROUP A - (Forwards):
Two forwards perform cover and attack movements in a field where there are four mannequins representing 4 opponent defenders. The mannequins are numbered 1 to 4 with one ball positioned next to them.

The Coach will call out number, forwards will move into their correct pressure positions. When the coach calls "GAME", the forward closest to the mannequin called, will take the ball, developing an attack on goal.

GROUP B - (Midfielders):
In a small field, such as displayed in the diagram, four red midfielders play against 4 blue midfielders. The blue team starts moving the ball from left to right simulating a switching play combination; the red team does the cover and attack movements.

When coach calls "GAME", there will be a fast game of 4v4; the team can score by stopping the ball in the end zone. When the goal-attempt finishes, the red team will start to move the ball and blue team will do the cover and attack movements.

Tactical Player Positioning and Ball Recovery

GROUP C - (Defenders):

Four defenders are positioned on their starting cone, approximately 7 yards away from the four boundary poles. The Coach starts by passing the ball in along the ground in any direction within the area.

The nearest player goes to ball, while the other three defenders get into good covering positions in relation to the ball.
The moment the defender receives the ball, the coach can ask for the players to stand still and coach the correct defensive line; cover, support and body shape/positioning.

The coach can progress this by serving the ball in the air to vary the defensive game situations.

Phase 2 of all 3 groups for better insight (See Diagram below):

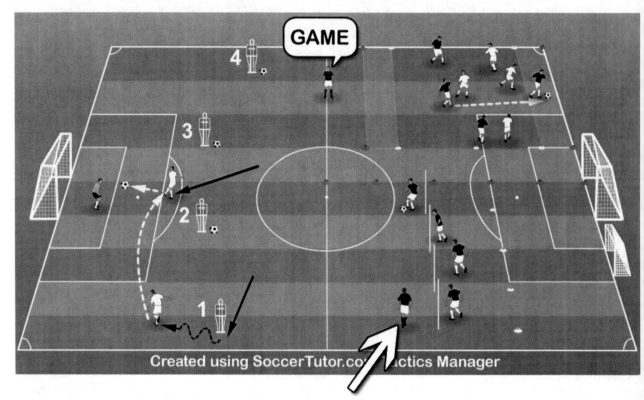

"GAME"
Coach stops the defenders and correct defensive line; cover, support and body shape/positioning

Real Game Attacking 2 v 1 Situations

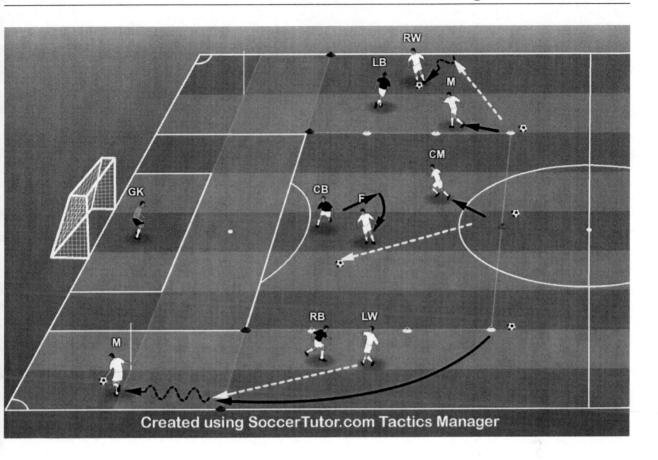

Created using SoccerTutor.com Tactics Manager

Objective
To reproduce real game situations in the attacking third of the pitch.

Description
Central zone of the field:
One central defender, plays against a midfielder (CM) and a forward (F) in a 2 v 1 duel. The game situation starts with CM passing to F with his back to goal to simulate a real match situation. The F and CM objective is to beat the defender and advance past 18 yard line where either one of them can shoot on goal unopposed.

Right and Left flank zones:
The full back ("defender") plays against the Winger (RW or LW) and Midfielder (M). The game situation starts with the 'M' passing to the winger whose objective is to beat the defender with an overlapping run or individually and advance past 18 yard line, go around the boundary pole and deliver a "cross" for the goalkeeper.

Coaching Points
1. The Forward and Wingers must create space by checking their run in the opposite direction before receiving the pass.
2. Angle of support, timing of runs and communication are crucial for 3rd man and overlapping runs.

Quick Play in a Small Sided Game

20 Minutes

Created using SoccerTutor.com Tactics Manager

Objective

To develop quick play in a very small sided game.

Description

Depending on how many players you have, deliberately set up a very small pitch.
The objective is to condense the space and encourage quick play.

Coaching Points

1. Encourage players to think and play quickly.
2. Correct body shape (open on the half-turn) and positioning is important to know where the next pass is going.
3. If tightly marked, players need to create space to get away from their opponent.

Session 5

Practice 1	Psycho-Kinetics (Think and Act Quickly) Warm-Up
Practice 2	Conditioning in a Technical Passing Exercise
Practice 3	Passing Practice for the Right Time of Play
Practice 4	Team Tactics - Possession and Defending
Practice 5	Small Sided Game Situations - 4 v 2 and 6 v 4
Practice 6	Psycho-Kinetics (Think and Act Quickly) Small Sided Game

Psycho-Kinetics (Think and Act Quickly) Warm-Up   10 Minutes

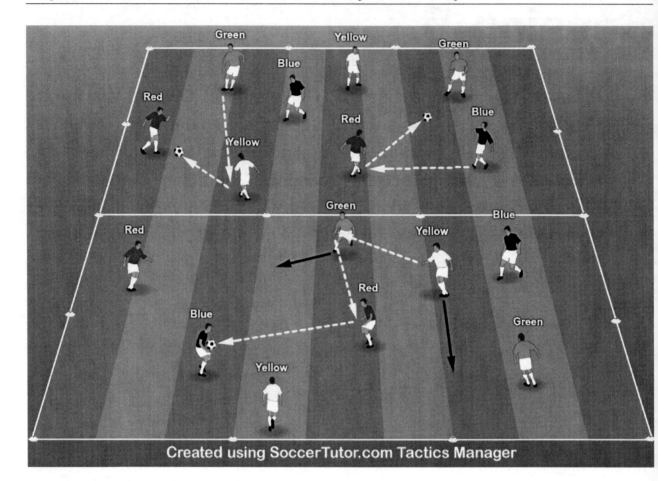

Created using SoccerTutor.com Tactics Manager

Objective
Develop your players to think and act quickly using Psycho-Kinetics.

Description
The team is divided into two groups of 8 players. Each group plays in their own area and the 8 players are allocated colours identified by training bibs/vests (2 Blue – 2 Red – 2 Green – 2 Yellow).

The players pass the ball by hand (throw and catch) trying to repeat all the logical sequence below which the coach dictates at any one time:

1. Pass the ball, calling the colour of the player receiving it
2. Pass the ball, calling the colour of the player receiving it (introducing 2 balls)
3. Pass the ball, calling a different colour of the player receiving it
4. Pass the ball, calling a colour. The player who receives the ball must pass to another player of the colour called from the player previously.
5. Pass the ball calling two different colours compared to the player receiving it.
6. Progress to passing with the feet, as shown in the diagram of the furthest group.

Conditioning in a Technical Passing Exercise

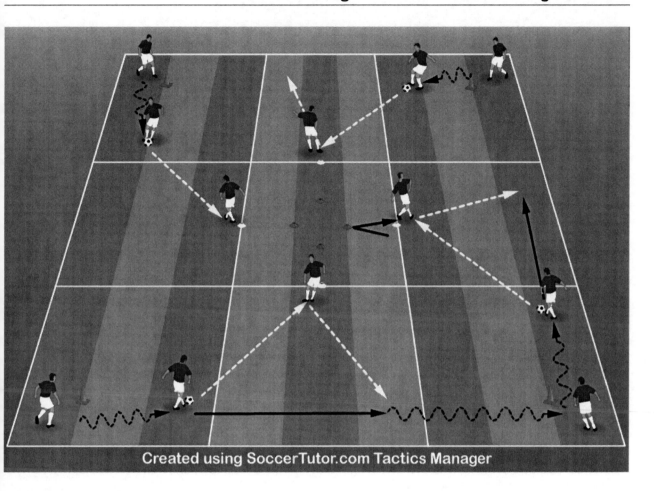

Created using SoccerTutor.com Tactics Manager

Objective
To develop both the technical aspects and the conditioning levels in a passing practice.

Description
Description
In a 30 x 30 yard area, four centre midfielders are inside the area, always moving. The midfielders will check back to the red cone before moving to meet the ball for the pass and perform a "give and go" with the other players who run with the ball.

Each player runs in a 30 yard circuit around the perimeter of the area with the ball at maximum speed.

Four balls are used simultaneously giving the spare player recovery time before receiving the ball.

Change the four players in the centre after 5 minutes.

Passing Practice for the Right Time of Play

20 Minutes

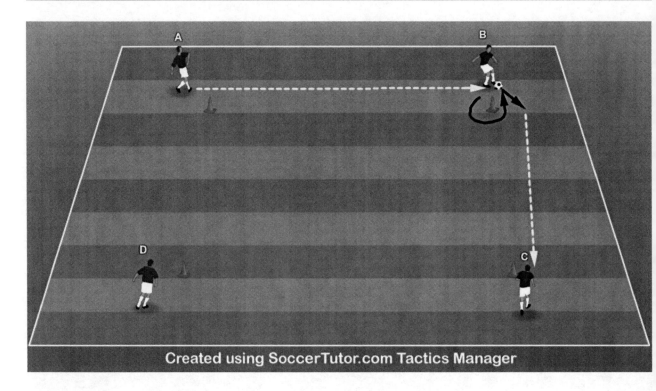

Created using SoccerTutor.com Tactics Manager

Objective
To improve passing at the right time of play.

Description
In football, passing at the right time and in the right way is very, very important. With this simple drill, we are going to work on both aspects:

Four players are positioned on all 4 corners of a square 1 yard away from the cones. The ball must always be out of the square moving in a circular way. Before the player receives the ball, he must go round on his cone clockwise, then passing the ball to his next team-mate.

Coaching Points
1. The crucial aspect of this drill is that all of the players time their run around the cone at the right time. If they delay, they will not receive the ball, if they do it in advance, they will wait for the ball and therefore the movement was not timed correctly.

2. When timing the run around the cone, keep the body open to see both the ball and the player.

3. It is important that players meet the ball and receive it with the back foot (the foot furthest away from the ball) this would put players automatically on the half-turn so

Team Tactics - Possession and Defending

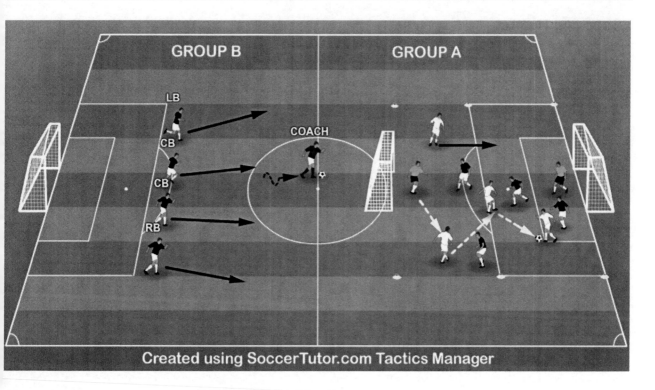

Created using SoccerTutor.com Tactics Manager

Objective

To develop team tactics for possession and the defensive line.

Description

Team is divided into two groups:

GROUP A:
(Forwards - Midfielders) Play a Small Sided Game of 4 v 4.
The objective is possession of the ball. The teams in possession can only score after 4 consecutive passes or more.

Variants of this game are:
- Condition the game with a maximum of 2 touches
- All the passes along the ground only, if the ball goes above knee height, possession of the ball changes.

GROUP B:
(Defenders) they work on the defensive line. "THE ELASTIC DEFEND" All four defenders respond to the coach's movement with the ball:
- If the coach advances with the ball, the DEFENSIVE LINE sprints backwards.
- If the coach runs with the ball in the opposite direction (as shown in the diagram), the DEFENSIVE LINE presses on.
- If the coach runs with the ball in laterally (left or right), the DEFENSIVE LINE stays compact.

Team Tactics - Possession and Defending

Coaching Points

1. 4 v 4 - Open body, create space, angle and support
2. Defenders - Run with short strides, communication is very impotant

Small Sided Game Situations - 4 v 2 and 6 v 4

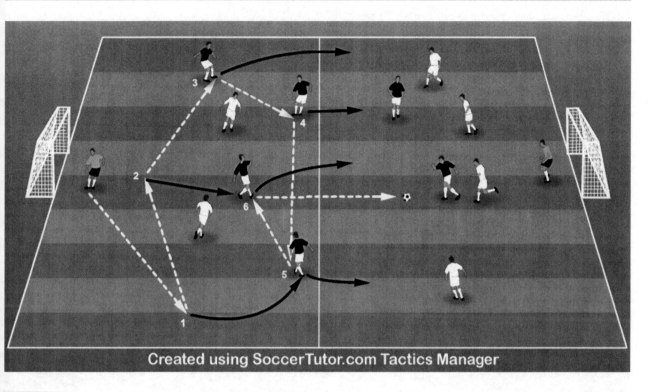

Created using SoccerTutor.com Tactics Manager

Objective

To develop possession in a small sided game situations.

Description

In a small field, the left half starts with a 4 v 2 situation. If four players make 5 consecutive passes or more they can enter (without pressure), the right half to create a 6 v 4 overload situation. The 6 players' objective is to score and the 4 players' to defend their goal.

If, in the left half, the 4 players fail to make 5 passes, possession will then start on the right half of the field, again with a 4 v 2 scenario.

Variations:
- Free touches
- Two touches
- Four players can be arranged in line or in a diamond

Coaching Points

1. Open body shape to see all playing options
2. Create space, moving at angles to support
3. Teach to the team the concept to maintain possession of the ball, finding the right time to shoot on goal

Psycho-Kinetics (Think and Act Quickly) Small Sided Game

15 Minutes

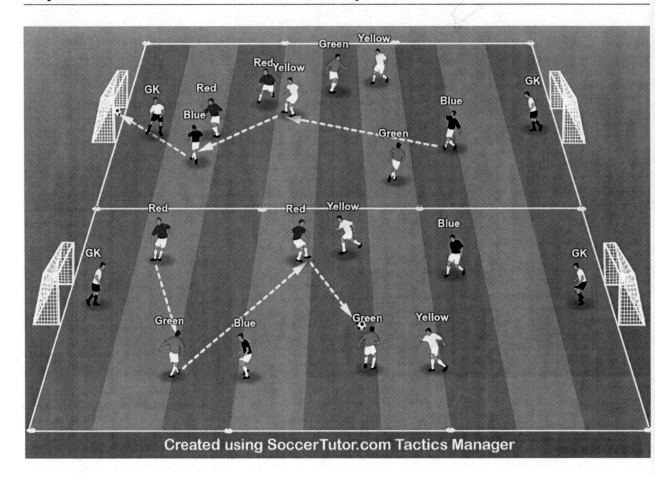

Created using SoccerTutor.com Tactics Manager

Objective

Develop your players to think and act quickly using Psycho-Kinetics in a small sided game.

Description

The team is divided into two groups of 8 players for 4 a-side where the Reds and Greens play against the Blues and Yellows identified by training bibs/vests. Playing with goalkeepers is optional.

Normal game except players cannot pass to the same colour within their own team. For example, Red player can only pass to Green player.

Coaching Points

1. Encourage players to think and play quickly selecting the right pass before receiving the ball.
2. Correct body shape (open on the half-turn) and positioning is important to know where the next pass is going.

Session 6

Psycho-Kinetics (Think and Act Quickly) Warm-Up   15 Minutes

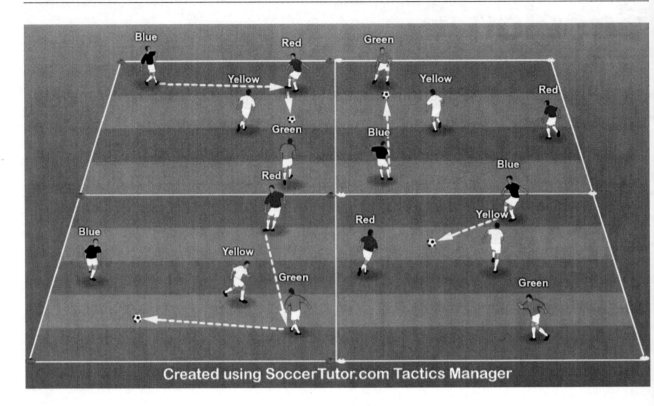

Created using SoccerTutor.com Tactics Manager

Objective

Develop your players to think and act quickly using Psycho-Kinetics.

Description

The team is divided into groups of four players each within a 10 x 10 yard area. Every player from each group has a different colour.

The game starts with players passing the ball by feet, calling the colour of the player who receives the ball. When the coach calls out a colour, example as shown in the diagram; "YELLOW" the players play 3 v 1 the colour called (YELLOW) becomes the player without the ball. When the colour touches the ball, the initial game restarts.

Coaching Points

1. Create space to find the right position on the field to receive the ball
2. Body shape and angle of support to receive and identify the next pass
3. Ask to play fast using only two touches where possible.
4. Reduce timing between the first touch (the receiving) and the second (passing)

20 Minutes

Explosive Power and Conditioning

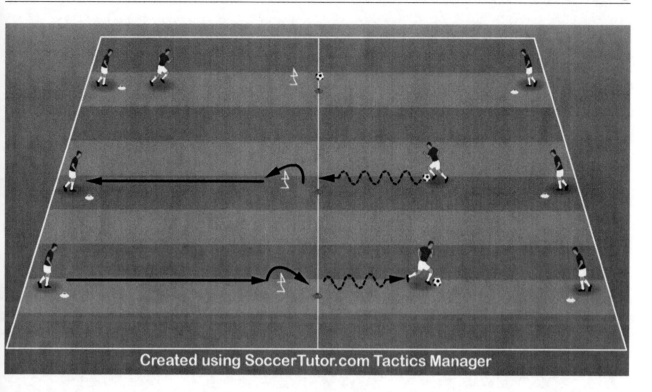

Created using SoccerTutor.com Tactics Manager

Objective
To develop explosive power and conditioning.

Description
Players are split up into groups of three (you can make one group of four if you don't have the right amount of players) with 2 players at one end and one player 50 yards away at the opposite end. A ball is positioned in the middle (25 yards away) and a hurdle which is 2 yards from the ball.

Left sided player
1. On the coach's command, players must sprint towards the hurdle (23 yards).
2. Jump over the hurdle (2 yards).
3. Take the ball and run with it to the opposite end (25 yards).

Right sided player
1. The single right sided player takes the ball from the left side player and runs towards the middle of the area (25 yards).
2. The player stops the ball on the centre line and jumps over the hurdle (2 yards).
3. The player then sprints (23 yards).

6 repetitions x 4 times
5 minutes: Stretching

Passing Practice for the Right Time of Play

15 Minutes

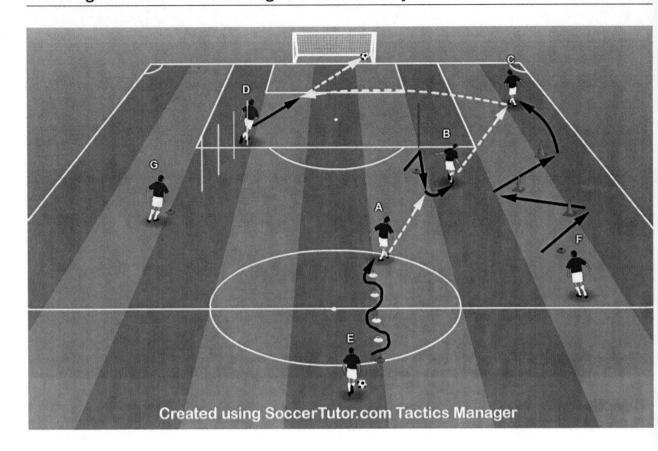

Objective
To improve passing at the right time of play.

Description
The midfielder (A) passes the ball to the forward (B) who checks to the red pole before receiving the ball. (B) then passes to the winger (C) who moves around the cones before crossing for the second forward (D) who in turn weaves in and out of the boundary poles before finishing on goal. Players rotate anti-clockwise.

The peculiarity of this exercise is that all the players must perform agility and coordination movements at the right time before advancing to the tactical combination.

All the defenders perform the technical circuit to improve their ball control.

Coaching Points
1. All the players should analyse all the team-mates movements on the field to gage the right time to time their run/movement.

20 Minutes

Team Tactics for Pressing and Covering Positioning

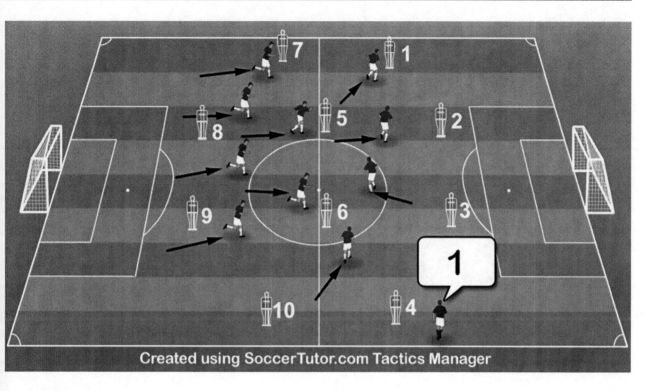

Created using SoccerTutor.com Tactics Manager

Objective

To develop team tactics for pressing and covering positioning (4-4-2 v 4-4-2).

Description

The team is lined up with a 4-4-2 system of play. In the field there are 10 mannequins (you can also use large cones) simulating the opponents (they are lined up in a 4-4-2 system of play too).

All the mannequins are numbered 1 to 10. The coach will randomly call out a number and the team will need to move, simulating the team cover in all three zones of the field.

Variations:

- The Coach can introduce a ball as a surprise addition to the drill. In this way, the team will pass with the intention of developing a counterattack or a combination on goal.

- Coach can move the mannequins to simulate different game situations:
  - If he moves the mannequins near the penalty his team's box, he can simulate a situation where the opponent team is doing the pressing.
  - If he moves the mannequins near the opposition's box, he can simulate a situation where his team is doing the pressing/forcing play.

Coaching Points

1. Encourage the attention of all the players to avoid bad positioning.
2. Avoid pressing too close to the opponent with both feet too square on.

Psycho-Kinetics Possession of the Ball - Dynamic Game

15 Minutes

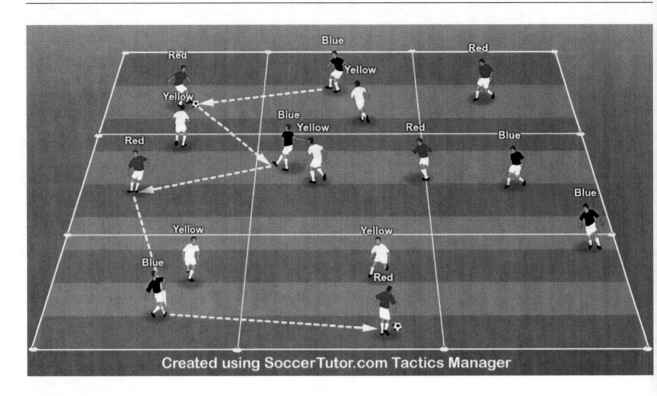

Created using SoccerTutor.com Tactics Manager

Objective

To develop possession of the ball using Psycho-Kinetics in a dynamic game.

Description

The team is divided into three colours inside a 30 x 30 yard area. This is a dynamic possession of the ball practice with a two colour team against a one colour team. If, for example, the Blue team loses possession, the game continues with the Red and Yellow trying to keep the ball with the blue trying to recover it.

As a coach you should try to enforce a conditional maximum of two touches only.

Coaching Points

1. Open body shape to see all of the playing options.
2. Play quickly (maximum of two touches) considering the overload of players.
3. If needed, create space to get away from the marker.

Psycho-Kinetics Possession of the Ball - With 3 Colours

Created using SoccerTutor.com Tactics Manager

Objective

To develop possession of the ball using Psycho-Kinetics in a dynamic game.

Description

In the same area as Practice 5 and with the same teams, this time the game is organised in the following way:

One color, for example the Red team, stays around the square playing (maximum of two touches) for the team that are in possession of the ball. Inside the area there are two colour teams; Blue and Yellow. One color has possession and tries to keep it. They can use the colour team around the square (Red team) for support. The other colour team (Yellow team) tries to win possession. Change the team on the outside every 3-4 minutes.

Variations:

- Free touches inside the square
- Two touches inside the square
- Two touches for all the players except the central midfielder's
- One touch for all

Session 7

20 Minutes

Warance-Up - Head Catch Small Sided Game

Created using SoccerTutor.com Tactics Manager

Objective
Develop heading and possession in a warm-up.

Description
In a field of 25 x 15 yards, organise three teams of 6 players each, with an optional addition of two goalkeepers (can use less depending on how many players you have). Two teams play inside, the other team is on outside of the area supporting the team in possession.

There are two different types of games:
1. 8 minutes: hands match, can only score by head; the team outside can play only by head
2. 8 minutes: all the teams can play only by head (only the first pass by hands). If the ball falls to the ground possession of the ball changes.

5 minutes stretching.

Coaching Points
1. Players within the field should always be moving
2. Check to create space to get away from marker

Football Specific Endurance Conditioning

15 Minutes

Created using SoccerTutor.com Tactics Manager

Objective

To develop football specific endurance conditioning whilst also working on technical passing.

Description

5 minutes: In a square 25 x 25 yards, two different teams (Blue and Yellow) pass the ball to each other. After the coach calls one team (for example "Yellow"), that team must immediately run to the boundary pole, touch it, and return inside the area with the objective to recover the ball.

At the same time the blue team will try to do 10 passes receiving one point if they achieve it before the last yellow player enters the area. Every 30 seconds there will be a call from the coach.

2 minutes: recovery

5 minutes: Interval training with ball each, 45 seconds dribbling with the ball slowly – 15 seconds running with the ball quickly

Technical - Crossing, Finishing and Passing

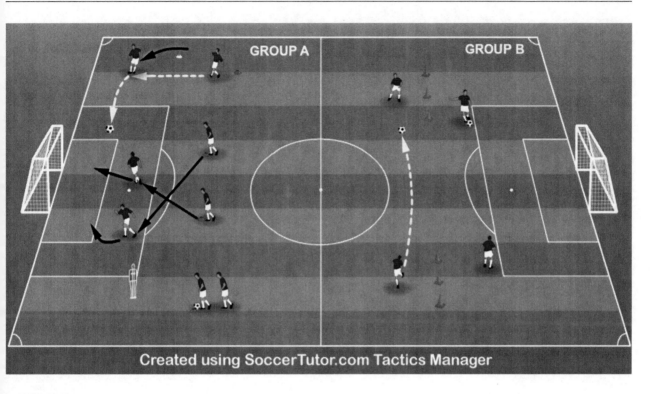

Created using SoccerTutor.com Tactics Manager

Objective
To develop crossing, finishing and passing techniques.

Description
The team is divided into two groups:

GROUP A: (left/right back, wingers and forwards)
In this drill, we are focusing on improving crossing technique and movement in the box. The left/right back and wingers take turns to cross the ball into the box where there are two forwards trying to finish after tactical movements (like crossing their runs). To improve the way the wingers cross the ball, the coach could suggest the following progressions:

- Cross after a move/feint using mannequin or pole/cone.
- Cross after a wall pass.
- Cross after an overlapping run.
- Practice from dead ball situations, like a free kick.

GROUP B (central defenders and central midfielders)
In this drill, players improve their long passing with both feet changing every time the distance between both players. In fact, after passing the ball, the player moves to another cone, ready to receive the pass from his teammate.

Technical - Crossing, Finishing and Passing

Coaching Points

1. Players crossing - Encourage variation: strong & fast, soft, along the ground, to the near post, to the far post.

2. The two forwards attacking the cross must time their runs well. Forwards must ensure they do not make their run too early. They should make it just when the wide player is about to cross it; this will prevent the ball going behind them.

3. The two forwards should communicate to tactically decide who will make their run to the near post, far post and if they are going to cross their runs or not.

4. Players passing - Quality of pass and variation i.e. driven pass (lower and fast), lofted pass (higher and slower).

20 Minutes

Crossing and Finishing in a Functional Practice

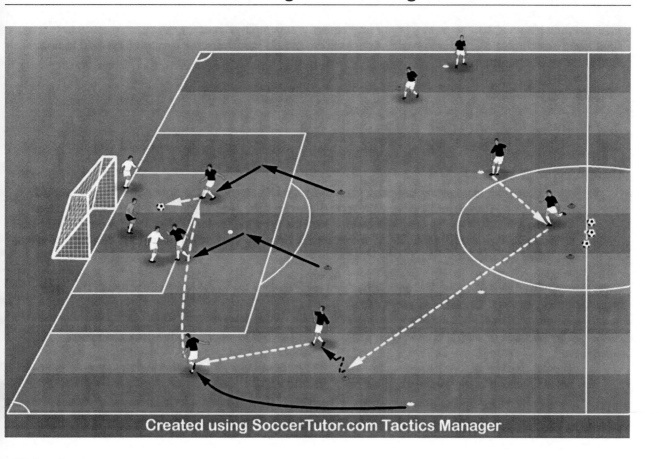

Created using SoccerTutor.com Tactics Manager

Objective
To develop crossing, finishing, passing and attacking movement.

Description
Similar set-up as the previous drill however the two central defenders are introduced. The 2 central midfielder's are positioned near the half-way line with one of the CM passing at an angle to the 2nd CM who takes a touch and delivers a long cross field pass to either the full back or winger who takes the ball inside and passes to the oncoming full back or winger who crosses in the box.

Different game situations:
10 minutes: There will be 2 forwards against 1 central defender. The defender marks one forward closely.

The cross will be delivered to the free forward.

10 minutes: 2 v 2 in the box. In this case there are 2 man to man marking in the box.

The coach can suggest some variations:
- Both defenders can start in the middle of the box
- Both defenders can start in the same line as the forwards
- One defender can start close to the near post and the second the far post

Crossing and Finishing in a Functional Practice

The central midfield (CM) role is very important aspect of training a soccer team.
After good ball control, a good cross requires a long cross field pass from the centre of the field to both lateral zones using both feet.

CM passing variations:
- Cross field driven pass along the ground
- Cross field driven pass along in the air
- Cross field lofted pass along in the air

Coaching Points

1. If the midfielder is receiving the pass from the 1st midfielder from the right side, then he should receive it with the left foot before delivering the cross field pass to the left. If receiving the pass from the left side, then he should receive it with the right foot before delivering the cross field pass to the right. This enables the CM to automatically open up the body facing in the direction of where to deliver the pass.

Note that the CM can deliver the ball with either foot regardless if it's to the left or right flank. The most important thing is which foot he receives it with.

2. The full back or winger should check to create space before receiving the crossfield pass.

3. The full back or winger receiving the cross field pass should take the ball inside to create space before passing to the overlapping full back or winger.

4. Players crossing - Encourage variation: strong & fast, soft, along the ground, to the near post, to the far post.

5. The two forwards attacking the cross must time their runs well. They must ensure against making their run too early. The forwards should make their run just as the wide player is about to cross the ball; this will prevent the ball going behind them.

6. The two forwards should communicate to tactically decide who will make their run to the near post, far post and if they are going to cross their runs or not.

Progression
After the 1st CM passes to the 2nd CM, he makes a run to the edge of the box to make a third attacking option

20 Minutes — **Team Tactics - Build-Up Play from the Back**

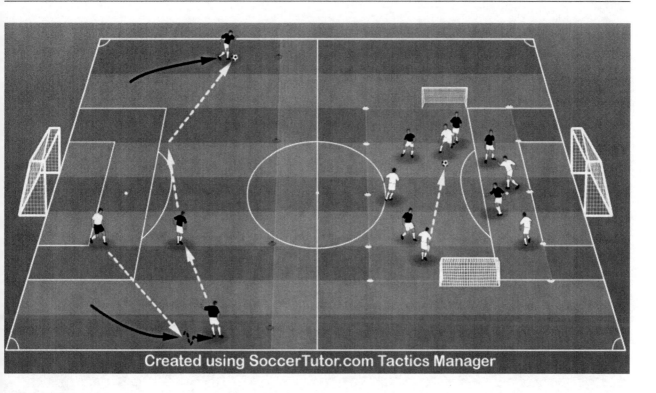

Created using SoccerTutor.com Tactics Manager

Objective
To develop team tactics with build-up play from the back.

Description
The first step involves the goalkeeper and the defensive line. The coach will work on developing build-up play with various switching play movements to develop the ball from the box to the halfway line.

When all the solutions are clear, the coach can introduce some opponents, (for example 2 or 3 forwards) and some new team-mates (one or two central midfielder's) for 6 v 2.

The rest of the team will play a free game in a small field.

Coaching Points
1. As soon as the GK receives the ball, the defenders should create space and adopt a good position by spreading out long and wide. The full backs should bend their runs. This creates space and makes it easier for the GK to distribute to.
2. For the 1st and most basic switch of play - Just when the full back turns with the ball, the 3 other defenders must drop back quickly in positions where the receiving player is behind the player with the ball.
3. All players must use the back foot when receiving the ball. This enables the players to automatically open up the body facing in the direction to pass the ball.

Overlaps in a Small Sided Game

15 Minutes

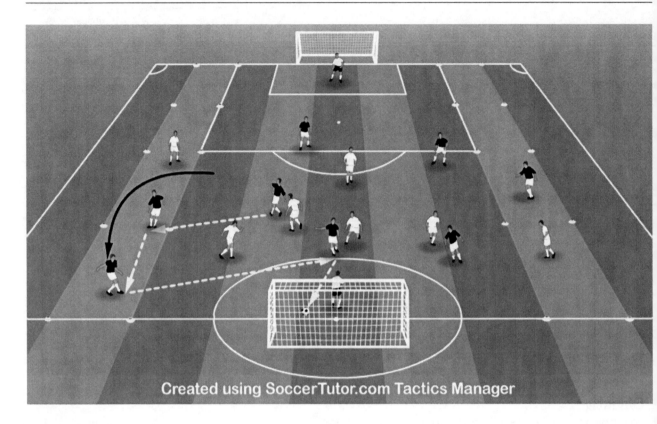

Created using SoccerTutor.com Tactics Manager

Objective

To improve the use of overlaps in a small sided game.

Description

Within half a field, there are two marked out flank zones where one player for both teams plays inside but cannot tackle the other. If a player passes to one of the flank players on their team, the same player or a teammate overlaps, crossing the ball and the team scores, it will count as 3 goals.

Game variations:
- Can only score by passing to a flank player first
- Can only score by making an overlap first
- When team scores, maintain possession and attack the opposite goal

Coaching Points
1. Make the overlapping runs at the right time of the game
2. The overlapping run must be timed well, communicating with the flank player as to when they should release the ball.
3. Forwards must try to reproduce all the correct movements in the box before attacking the cross.

Session 8

Technical Heading, Control and Balance Warm-Up

15 Minutes

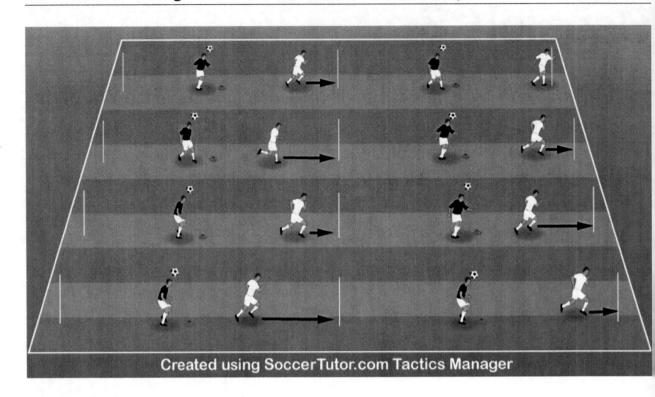

Created using SoccerTutor.com Tactics Manager

Objective

To develop heading, control and balance in a warm-up.

Description

Description

Players are divided into pairs with 1 ball and named Player "A" and Player "B". The players have to perform one of the following sequences:

- Player "A" juggles the ball with the head, afour touches he passes the ball to Player "B" for the same sequence.
- Same as above but whilst sitting on the ground
- Player "A" heads with one touch, player "B" two touches
- Players head the ball to each other, one touch only
- Players head the ball to each other - two touches

During this time the coach will call out either "A" or "B", at which point this player has to immediately run around the boundary pole and back again.

The coach can instruct the players to move around the boundary pole in the following ways:

- Jogging/sprinting forwards, both backwards and laterally
- Skipping, knees up and butt-kicks

Stretch after 5, 10 and 15 minutes

15 Minutes

Explosive Power in a 1 v 1 Situation

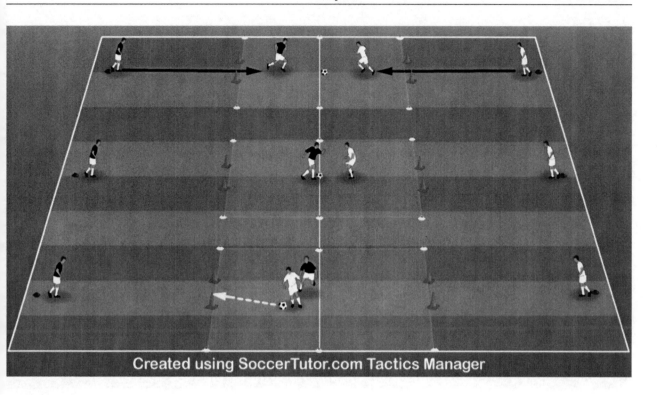

Created using SoccerTutor.com Tactics Manager

Objective

To develop explosive power in a 1 v 1 situation.

Description

Players play 1 v 1 in an area of 10 x 15 yards.

When the coach calls the player's number (i.e. "2"), the numbered player from each end sprints a distance of 15-20 yards where a ball is positioned at the centre of the playing area.

The first player who gets to the ball has an objective to beat the opponent and score in the small goal.

As soon as the ball goes out of bounds or a goal is scored, the player must retrieve the ball and position it back in the centre of the area ready for the next set of players.

Before the players start the above 1 v 1, they need to perform the following:
- Three squat jump series – a series being six seconds in a squat position before jumping ten times.
- Hurdle circuit with four medium hurdles: 5 repetitions (see diagram 2)
- Hurdle circuit with four high hurdles: 5 repetitions (see diagram 2)
- 10 metre jumping run

For hurdle circuits, see *diagram 2* of following page.

Explosive Power in a 1 v 1 Situation

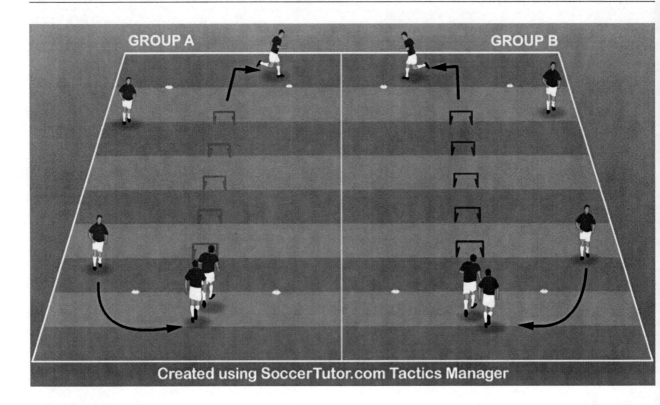

Description

BPlayers are split into 2 groups.

Group A:
Players line up in front of medium size hurdles. The players jump two-footed over the hurdles and then jog right, towards the start of the large (high) hurdles.

Group B:
Players line up in front of large (high) size hurdles. The players jump two-footed over the hurdles and then jog left, towards the start of the medium size hurdles.

Both groups do five repetitions of each sized hurdle.

Technical Heading in Pairs

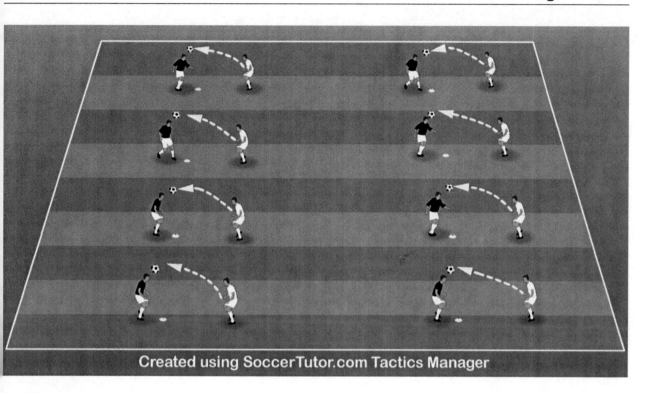

Created using SoccerTutor.com Tactics Manager

Objective
To develop heading technique.

Description
Players are divided into pairs with one ball and named Player "A" and Player "B".
The players have to perform one of the following sequences:
- 30 Headers - without jumping
- 30 Headers - jumping with both feet at the same time
- 30 Headers - jumping to the left and to the right (simulating a pendulum)
- 30 Headers - lunging at the ball
- 30 Headers - running in the opposite direction of the ball

Coaching Points
1. Control the correct use of both arms (before connecting with the ball, during connection with the ball and after).
2. Control the jump before connecting with the ball (using the right leg to take off).
3. Establish the right way to run before connecting with the ball.

Attacking Heading Game

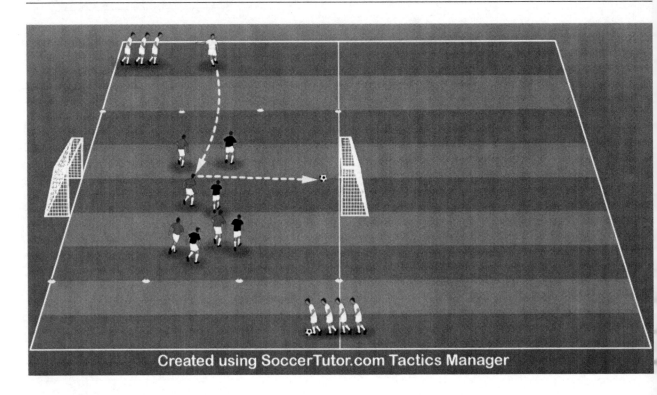

Created using SoccerTutor.com Tactics Manager

Objective

To develop heading inside the penalty area.

Description

Within the penalty area, eight players play 4 v 4 with a man-to-man marking situation.

All the other players will stay outside; taking turns to cross the ball inside the area from both the right and left flanks. Teams earn 2 points by scoring with the head and 1 point scoring with a volley.

Players switch round after 7 minutes.

Coaching Points

Attacking:
1. Anticipate where the ball will be delivered, however try to time the run so that the ball can be attacked from the front and not go behind.
2. Try to lose your marker, i.e. fake to go near post but check back and move to the far post or a central position.

Defending:
1. Establish the correct position for the defender to take up (always between the forward and the goal).
2. Man-to-man marking inside the box during the game (change the marking after five times)

20 Minutes   **Team Tactics - Build-Up Play from the Back**

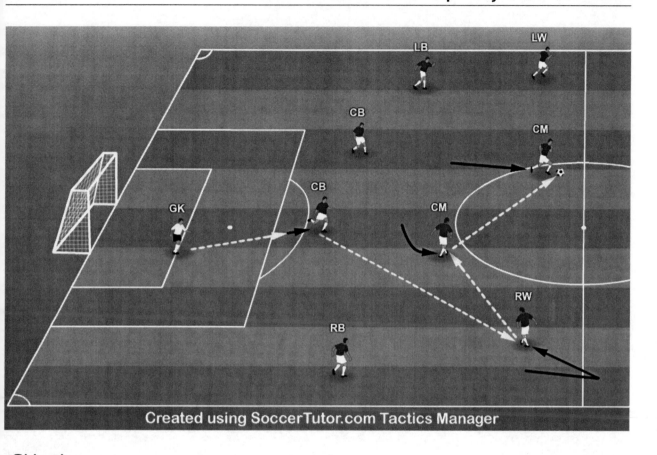

Created using SoccerTutor.com Tactics Manager

Objective
To develop team tactics with build-up play from the back.

Description
This is a progression from the previous session 7, practice 5. This time, we will involve 4 defenders (the defensive line) and 4 midfielders (the midfielder line).

The coach will ask the players to develop build-up play up to the halfway line with different kinds of combinations.

Example 1 - Diagram 1:
The goalkeeper passes the ball the to the central defender. He drives the ball into the path of the right winger that is running towards the ball after creating space.

The winger, with only one touch, passes the ball to the central midfielder nearest to, and behind him.

The combination ends with a pass from one central midfielder to the other.

Team Tactics - Build-Up Play from the Back

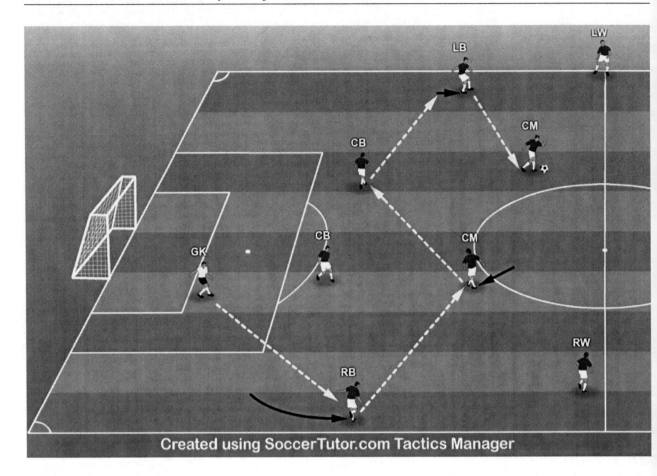

Created using SoccerTutor.com Tactics Manager

Example 2 - Diagram 2:
The goalkeeper passes the ball the right back that passes to the right central midfielder, who in turn, passes immediately to the left central defender.

Seeing the left back's movement, he passes the ball to him and on receipt of the pass the left back passes the ball to the central midfielder who advances towards the half-way line.

Coaching Points
1. Anticipate where the ball will be delivered, however try to time the run so the ball can the attacked from the front and not does not behind.
2. Try losing your marker, i.e. fake to go near post but check back and go middle or far post.

20 Minutes

Build-Up Play in a Small Sided Game

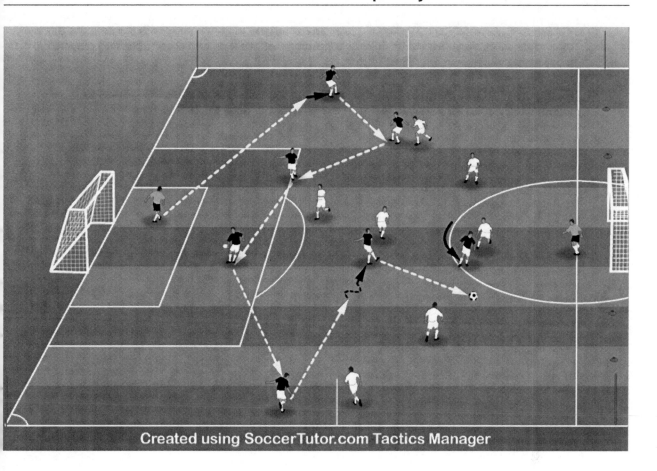

Created using SoccerTutor.com Tactics Manager

Objective
To develop team tactics with build up play from the back.

Description
Every two minutes, the coach will ask the players to try some combinations. For example, the blue team has the ball; they try to develop a build-up play combination starting from their goalkeeper.

When the ball is inside the blue half, the red team will be passive (not allowed to tackle); as soon as the ball crosses the halfway line, the real game starts. After 2 free game minutes, the red team will start a combination from their goalkeeper.

Coaching Points
1. Play and think quickly
2. As soon as the GK receives the ball, the defenders should create space and adopt a good position by spreading out long and wide.
   The full backs should bend their run. This creates space and makes it easier for the GK to distribute to the players.

Build-Up Play in a Small Sided Game

3. For the first and most basic switch of play - just when the full back turns with the ball, the three other defenders must drop back quickly in positions where they can cover attacking players' movements.

4. All players must use the back foot when receiving the ball. This enables the players to automatically open up the body facing in the direction to pass the ball.

Session 9

Possession and Transition Warm-Up

15 Minutes

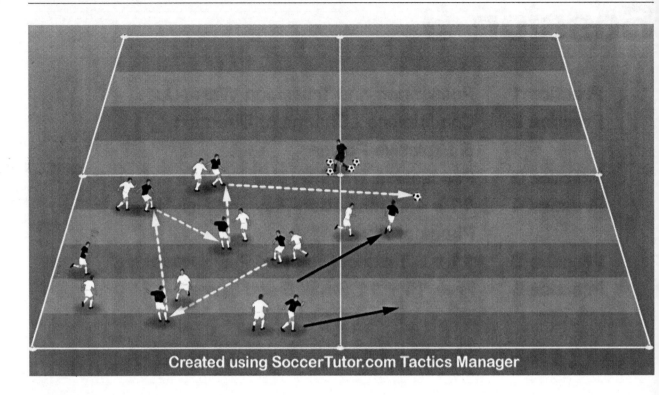

Created using SoccerTutor.com Tactics Manager

Objective
To develop possession of the ball and transitions with long passes.

Description
Players are divided into two groups.

The object of the game is to keep the possession of the ball in a field composed of four squares. Possession starts in one of the squares. After five passes, the team with the ball must transition to another square with a long pass. In this case, it is important that after the fourth pass, one or more players will make a run to another square, ready to receive the long pass.

The coach will be in the middle of this field with some balls. He can decide whether to introduce another ball into the field changing exercise when he wants and also make adjustments to the size of the square and the particular game situation the practice is simulating.

Stretch after 5 and 15 minutes

Coaching Points
1. Players should always be moving
2. Body shape should be open on half-turn to see all players.
3. If marked, create space to get away from marker
4. Players making runs forward to receive long pass should anticipate the pass by curving their run.
5. Good communication

Conditioning - Change of Direction & Explosive Power

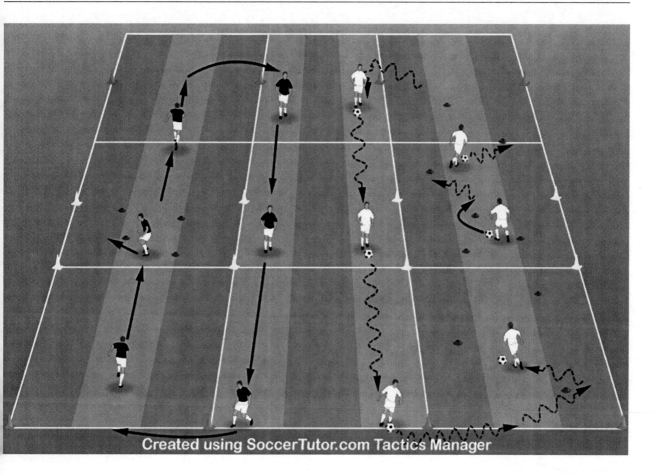

Created using SoccerTutor.com Tactics Manager

Objective
To develop change of direction, acceleration and explosive power.

Description
Group A (Without a ball):
- 10 yard straight sprint
- 5 yard walking pace side-to-side movement
- 10 yard straight sprint again
- Five repetitions.

Group B (With a ball):
- 10 yard running with the ball with quick change of direction
- 5 yard close ball control using cones to make feints
- 10 yard running with the ball with quick change of direction
- Five repetitions.

Both groups slowly jog/dribble back to start. After 5 repetitions they change sides.

Possession and Interplay

15 Minutes

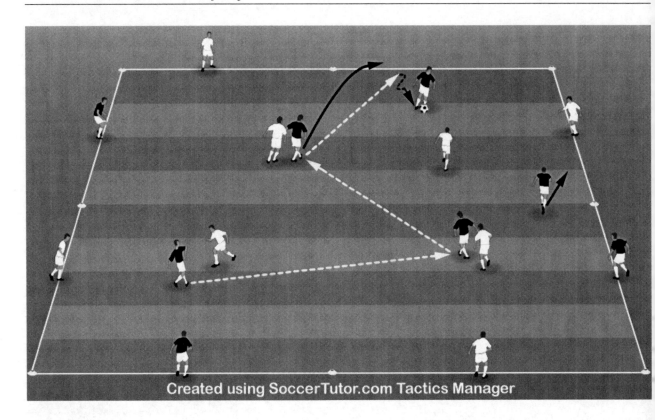

Created using SoccerTutor.com Tactics Manager

Objective

To develop possession of the ball and interplay.

Description

In a 25 x 25 yard square there are two teams of 8 players each.

There will be 4 v 4 players inside the square and 4 players from each team, evenly spread on the outside along all sides of the square.

The players inside must keep the ball using the players outside of the square on the same team.

When there is a pass to one player outside, this player will receive and run with the ball inside the square. The players who makes the pass, changes places on the outside.

Coaching Points

1. Body shape should be open on half-turn to see all players.
2. If marked, create space to get away from marker
3. Players making the pass to outside player should not run across his path. His run should be a curved run behind the player running inside with the ball.
4. Play quickly with all players (inside and outside) moving and showing for the ball.

Variation:

Coaches can insert two midfielders with another colour that will play with both teams but with only one touch.

11 v 4 Combination Play and Finishing in a Phase of Play

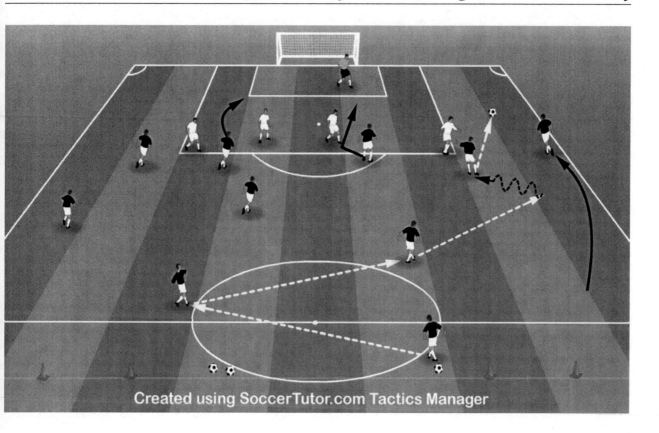

Created using SoccerTutor.com Tactics Manager

Objective
To develop combination play, possession of the ball and finishing.

Description
On just over half a field, a team of 11 play against 4 back line defenders.

The objective for the team of 11 is to develop the "combination of play with the aim of finishing on goal".

The back line of four defenders tries all the correct defensive movements.
If they win the ball, they must aim for the 2 target goals.

Coaching Points
1. Must develop good possession of the ball
2. Must play quickly with one or two touches

Progression
1. Introduce two more defensive players, playing 11 v 6 (See following phase of play).

11 v 6 Combination Play and Finishing in a Phase of Play   15 Minutes

Created using SoccerTutor.com Tactics Manager

Objective
To develop combination play, possession of the ball and finishing.

Description
On just over half a field a team of 11 play against four back line defenders and two defensive midfielders.

Again, the objective for the team of 11 is to develop the "combination of play with the aim of finishing on goal".

The six defensive players try to stop them from playing. If they win the ball, they must try to make 5 consecutive passes and then aim for the 2 target goals.

Coaching Points
1. Body shape should be open on half-turn to see all players.
2. If marked, create space to get away from marker
3. Must play quickly with one or two touches

Progression
1. Introduce two more defensive players, playing 11 v 8 (See following phase of play).

11 v 6 Combination Play and Finishing in a Phase of Play

Created using SoccerTutor.com Tactics Manager

Description
Another two players are introduced to make 11 v 8. This means we now have four defenders and four midfielders.

Objective for the team of 11 is to develop the "combination of play with the aim of finishing on goal".

Go through different combinations of play with your players before allowing them to play freely.

The eight players try to win the ball. They must try to make five consecutive passes and then aim for the 2 target goals.

Coaching Points
1. Go through different combinations of play with your players before allowing them to play freely.
2. Body shape should be open on half-turn to see all players
3. If marked, create space to get away from marker
4. Must play quickly with one or two touches

Free 11 v 11 Small Sided Game

20 Minutes

Created using SoccerTutor.com Tactics Manager

Objective

To enhance the attributes that have been worked on in previous practices such as possession, transition and combination/build up play from the back.

Description

Play 11 v 11. If you haven't got that many players, then simply play with the numbers you have, I.e. 7 v 7 etc.

Coaching Points

1. Focus on the attributes you worked on in the previous practices such as possession, transition and combination/build up play from the back.
2. When you see a mistake, stop the game and ask the players what they could have done better and what other options they had. Players should then rehearse the better option and then play live.

Session 10

Two Group Possession and Finishing Warm-Up

15 Minutes

Created using SoccerTutor.com Tactics Manager

Objective

To develop possession of the ball and finishing in a warm-up.

Description

The team is divided into two groups:

GROUP A: (Forwards):

Shooting in the box. Each forward takes turn to shoot on goal from alternate sides.
(8 -10 balls consecutively).

Variants:

- Shooting – ball on the ground
- Shooting – ball bouncing
- Shooting – ball in the air (volley)
- Receiving and shooting - ball on the ground
- Receiving and shooting - ball bouncing
- Receiving (by chest) and shooting - ball in the air

GROUP B:

(Rest of the team). 6 v 6 in a small sided game. The objective is to keep possession of the ball. Both teams can only score after 5 passes.

Two Group Possession and Finishing Warm-Up

Coaching Points

Forwards:

1. Evaluate the positions of the opposing defence before shooting on goal.
2. Positive attitude to hit the target
3. Value the right position of the support foot closest to goal.
4. Value the chest position to avoid kicking the ball over the goal

Small Sided Possessions Game:

1. Body shape should be open on half-turn to see all players.
2. If marked, create space to get away from marker.
3. Play quickly.

Endurance and Speed Training With/Without the Ball

20 Minutes

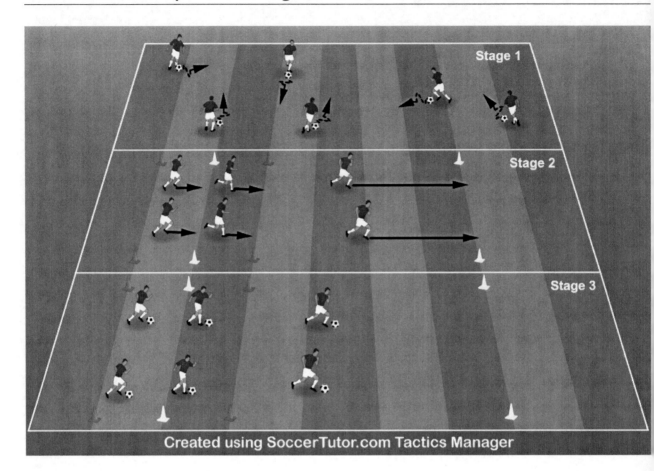

Stage 1

Stage 2

Stage 3

Created using SoccerTutor.com Tactics Manager

Objective

To develop endurance and speed training with and without the ball.

Description

1. **5 minutes** – Running with a ball at 80% of maximum intensity
2. **3 minute**s – Stretching
3. **Special sprint *without a ball*** - (5 yards),
    Slow jog – (5 yards), then 20 yards of sprinting 5 times (recovery time 45 seconds) for three repetitions (recovery time 3 minutes between each repetition).
4. **3 minutes** stretching
5. **30 yards skip run** (changing the way of skip)
6. **Special sprint *with a ball*** - 5 yards, slow dribble -dribble - 5 yards, then 20 yards sprint) five times (recovery time 45 seconds) with three repetitions (recovery time 3 minutes between each repetition)

15 Minutes

Anticipation and Intercepting the Ball

Created using SoccerTutor.com Tactics Manager

Objective
To develop anticipating the speed of the ball and interception.

Description
The team is divided into groups of three players.

Player (A) is positioned on a red cone behind Player (B) positioned 3 yards ahead.

Player (C) is positioned with a ball 8 yards away with a yellow and blue cone positioned 3 yards away from the red cone.

Player (C) starts by passing the ball towards Player (B). Just as the pass is made,
Player (A) needs to quickly evaluate the speed of the ball and decide to make an interception or wait.

If Player (A) anticipates and decides to make the interception, he must receive and pass back to Player (C).

If Player (A) decides to wait, he must defend and prevent Player (B) from passing back to Player (C) only after Player (B's) first touch.

Anticipation and Intercepting the Ball

After 8 minutes:

After Player (C) passes; he must move to either the blue or yellow cone and receive the pass back from either Player (A) or Player (B).

Coaching Points

1. Player (A) needs to evaluate the speed of the ball to decide either back-marking or anticipating and intercepting the pass.
2. Use the foot closer to the opponent for correct interception
3. Use the arm closer the opponent to help get in front of him

Game Situations - Feinting and Finishing

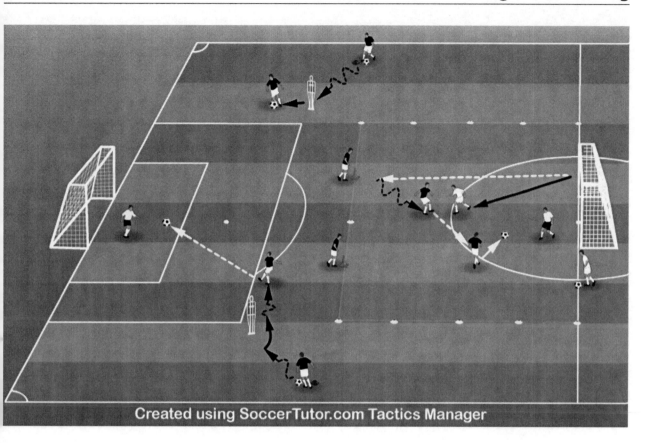

Created using SoccerTutor.com Tactics Manager

Objective
To develop feinting and finishing in game situations.

Description
Team is divided into two groups.

GROUP A (Full Backs and Wingers)
Players start from the flanks, dribble the ball towards the mannequin, and then must make a feint, and shoot on goal, going one time inside the centre of the field and one time outside the centre of the field.

GROUP B (Rest of the team)
2 v 1 game situation in the central zone.
The central defenders will defend against the two centre forwards or midfielders.

Coaching Points
1. Dribble the ball with many touches
2. Try to shoot on goal immediately after the feint.
3. Keep the ball close to the feet whilst dribbling
4. Use both feet to shoot on goal

Attacking Combinations of Play and Finishing

20 Minutes

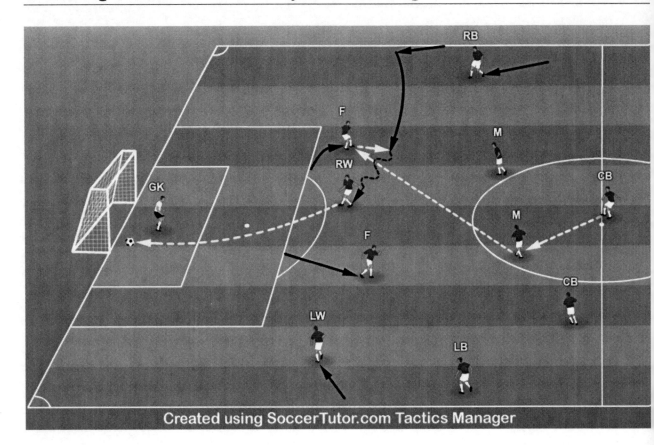

Created using SoccerTutor.com Tactics Manager

Objective

To develop combinations of play and finishing in the final phase.

Description

The team is set up unopposed in their playing positions.

Starting from the halfway line, the team will develop some combinations of play with the objective of shooting on goal.

With the "final phase" we want to work on many different attacking combinations to finish on goal.

One example:

After receiving from the centre back, the central midfielder plays the ball for the opposite forward.

After receiving, the forward passes the ball to the right winger who makes a run inside and follows with a strike on goal.

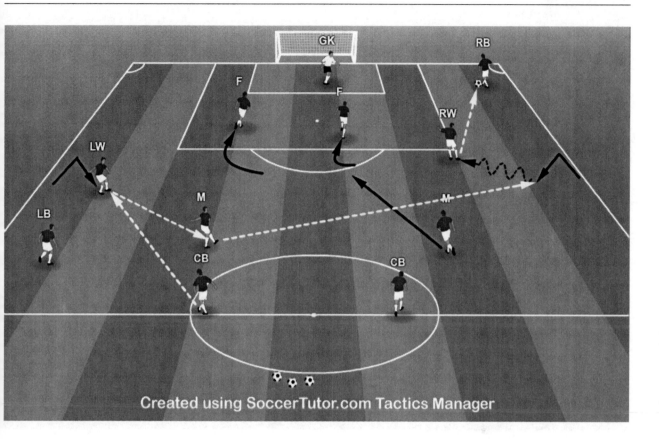

Created using SoccerTutor.com Tactics Manager

Description

The centre back passes to the left winger who checks before receiving the ball, passing inside to the centre midfielder.

The Midfielder quickly switches play to the right winger who moves inside to meet the ball, then dribbles inside to create the space for the overlapping right back.

The right back crosses for both forwards who make a run to the near and far post. The second Midfielder makes a run to the edge of the penalty area for a pull-back or to pick up on any loose balls.

The left winger should also make a run around the back to anticipate a cross that may be over-hit.

Variation 2

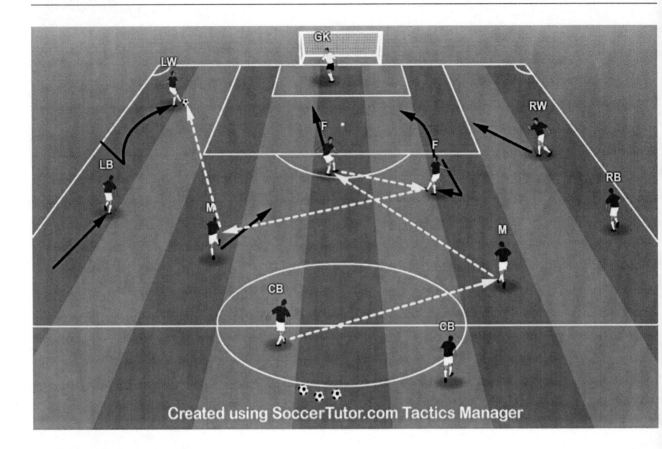

Description

The centre back passes to the centre midfielder who quickly passes to the furthest forward. During this time the second forward makes a run to receive the ball short.

The ball is played on to the second striker with a first touch by the player furthest forward.

The forward in turn, checks back to receive the ball and play it first-time to the midfielder.

The Midfielder passes forward to the left winger who will cross for the ball for the forwards making runs to the near and far post. The second midfielder makes a run to the edge of the penalty area for any rebounds.

The right winger should also make a run around the back to anticipate a cross that may be over-hit.

Coaching Points

1. Timing of runs - Players must move at the right time of play, understanding all of the movements of all their team-mates.
2. Body shape - Orientate the body, before receiving the ball, trying to get sight of the opponent's goal as quickly as possible.
3. Play one or two touches.

Possession and Build-Up Play in a Small Sided Game

Created using SoccerTutor.com Tactics Manager

Objective

To work on possession, the tactical build up play and finishing that have been worked on in previous practices.

Description

Play 11 v 11.
If you haven't got that many players, then simply play with the numbers you have,
I.e. 7 v 7 etc.

Coaching Points

1. Think and Play quickly
2. Try to maintain the possession of the ball

Session 11

Two Group Ball Control and Shooting Warm-Up

Created using SoccerTutor.com Tactics Manager

Objective
To develop shooting, ball control, dribbling and quick change of direction.

Description
The team is divided into two groups:

GROUP A: (Forwards):
Shooting in the box - This time the ball will be thrown by both corners of the box.
The forward aims to strike on goal, keeping the ball as close to the ground as possible.

GROUP B: (Rest of the team):
Dribble the ball with a 25 x 25 yard area.

Variants:
- Right foot only
- Left foot only
- Alternating quickly - inside left and inside right
- Using both soles of the feet
- Right foot only, one inside, one outside
- Left foot only, one inside, one outside
- Dribbling and change of direction using the inside foot close to a team-mate
- Dribbling and change of direction using the outside foot close to a team-mate

Two Group Ball Control and Shooting Warm-Up

Coaching Points

Forwards:

1. Positive attitude to hit the target
2. Value the right position of the support foot closest to the goal
3. Value the chest position to avoid kicking the ball over the goal

Technical Ball Control (Dribbling and quick change of direction):

1. Dribble with many quality touches of the ball
2. Keep the ball close to the feet
3. Soft touch with the ball

Speed Training

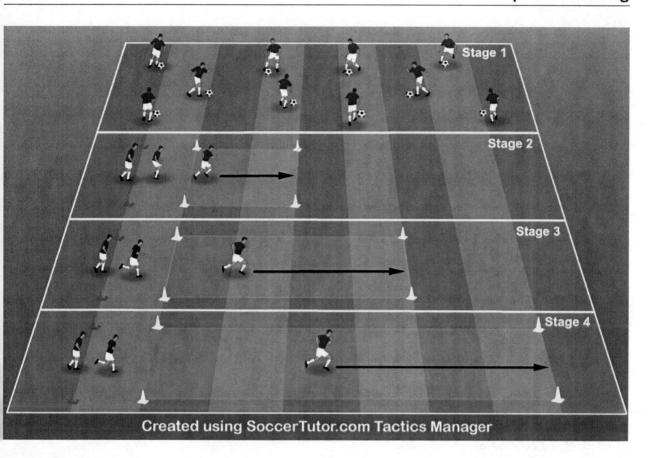

Stage 1

Stage 2

Stage 3

Stage 4

Created using SoccerTutor.com Tactics Manager

Objective
To develop speed training without the ball.

Description
1. **5 minutes** (Stage 1) – Dribbling with a ball at half pace
2. (Stage 2) 10 x 10 yard sprints
3. (Stage 3) 10 x 20 yard sprints
4. (Stage 4) 10 x 30 yard sprints
5. **5 minutes** – Stretching

Quick Inter-Play, Finishing & Individual Defending

Created using SoccerTutor.com Tactics Manager

Objective

Group A - To develop finishing after quick inter-play.
Group B - To develop frontal marking/defending.

Description

Team is divided into two groups.

GROUP A (Midfielders and Forwards):

Players will vary different quick combinations of play with the objective of quickly shooting on goal.

Below is the first example (see above diagram) of three:

1. The central midfielder passes the ball to the opposite forward. He quickly meets the ball and passes to the other midfielder who times his run well and strikes on goal.

The second forward needs to get into a good position to receive a possible through pass and also follow in on any rebounds from the goalkeeper.

Quick Inter-Play, Finishing & Individual Defending

Second example (see diagram below) of three:

2. The winger passes the ball to the nearest forward. If the winger makes a run inside the field, the forward will pass the ball to him and the winger will shoot on goal.

The second forward needs to get into a good position to receive a possible through pass and also follow in on any rebounds from the goalkeeper.

GROUP B (Defenders):
All the defenders will play a 1 vs1 situation. The focus is on working on frontal marking.

Quick Inter-Play, Finishing & Individual Defending

Third example (see diagram below) of three:

3. If the winger makes a run on the flank, he will deliver a floated ball across the box for both of the forwards.

Created using SoccerTutor.com Tactics Manager

GROUP B (Defenders)

All the defenders will play a 1 vs 1 situation. The focus is working on frontal marking.

Coaching Points

GROUP A (Midfielders and Forwards):

1. Timing - Make all the actions at the right time of play
2. Body shape - All the players must receive the ball in a position that enables them to have the best peripheral vision
3. When possible, receive the ball in the space; this way the actions can be faster.

GROUP B (Defenders):

1. Assess the opponent's speed
2. Running speed of the defender, slowing down before approaching
3. Position of both feet of the defender, the optimum is for defenders to always have a foot in front, never with both feet in the same line (also known as the 'Jockey' or 'surfer' position).
4. The defender must direct the forward onto his weaker foot

15 Minutes

Game Situations - Individual Tactics, Counter-attacking and Finishing

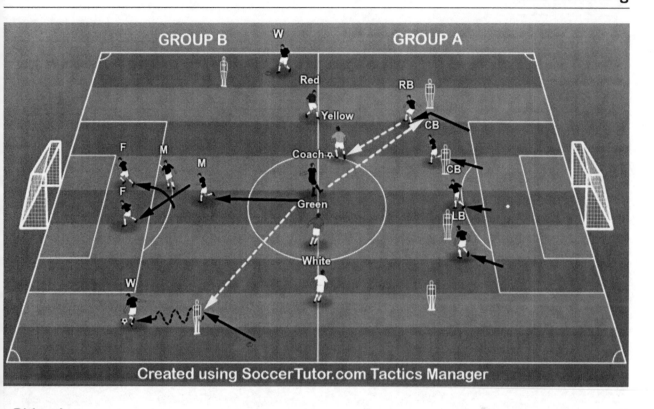

Created using SoccerTutor.com Tactics Manager

Objective
To develop individual tactics in game situations, such as anticipation, quick counterattacking, attacking and finishing.

Description
Team is divided into two groups.

GROUP A (Back line Defenders and 4 Midfielders):
The defenders line up in a defensive line of four players behind 4 mannequins.
Four different colour midfielders (red, yellow, green and white) are positioned on the halfway line.

The coach will start the exercise by passing the ball along the ground towards one of the four mannequins.
As in a game situation, the defender will try to "anticipate" the pass, intercepting it and pass to the right colour simulating a counterattack.
The colour will be called by the coach.

Variations:
1. The coach will try different anticipations with the ball on the ground and the ball in the air.

Game Situations - Individual Tactics, Counter-attacking and Finishing

2. In this second variation *(see diagram below):*

After the coach passes, he will give a special signal, for a 4 v 4 situation (four coloured midfielders vs. four defenders).

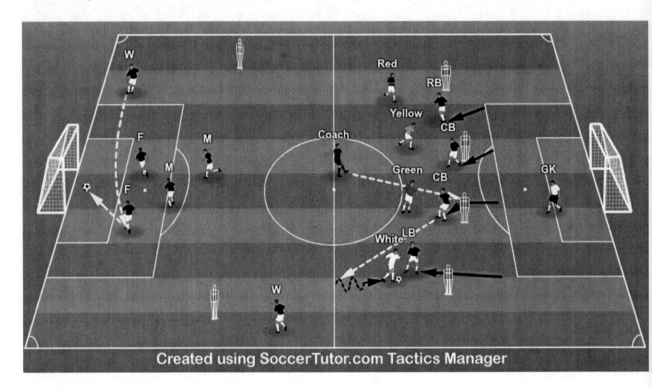

Created using SoccerTutor.com Tactics Manager

GROUP B (Forwards, Wingers and 2 Midfielders):
The midfielder passes the ball out wide and the winger has to anticipate the pace of the ball, getting in front of the mannequin before advancing to deliver a floated ball inside the box where there will be both forwards and one central midfielder.
The other central midfielder will stay out of the box, ready to shoot on goal.

Coaching Points
GROUP A
1. Players should assess the ball speed to choose to do a back marking or anticipation.
2. Use the foot closer to the opponent to accurately anticipate their movement and intercept the ball.
3. Use the arm closer to the opponent to "enter" in front of him
4. The pass, before counterattacking, must be fast and then all the defensive line must squeeze up.

Attacking Combination Play and Finishing - 10 v 4

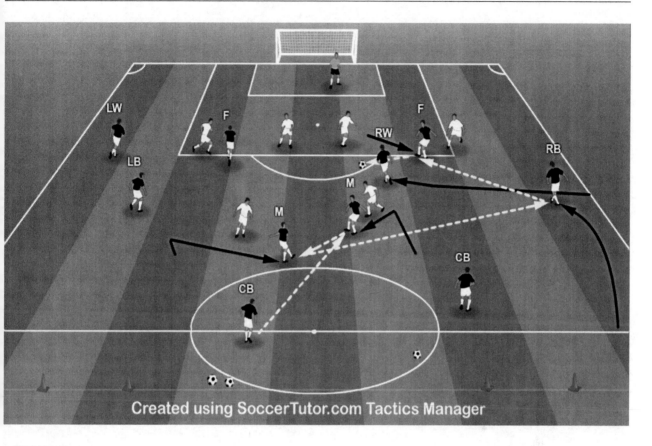

Created using SoccerTutor.com Tactics Manager

Objective

To develop attacking combination play with the emphasis to shoot on goal – system of play 4-4-2

Description

The team will try all the final step combinations to shoot on goal.
- First 10 minutes will be 4 defenders and 2 midfielders
- Last 10 minutes will be 4 defenders and 4 midfielders -
  (see diagram on next page):

Attacking Combination Play and Finishing - 10 v 4

- Last 10 minutes will be 4 defenders and 4 midfielders

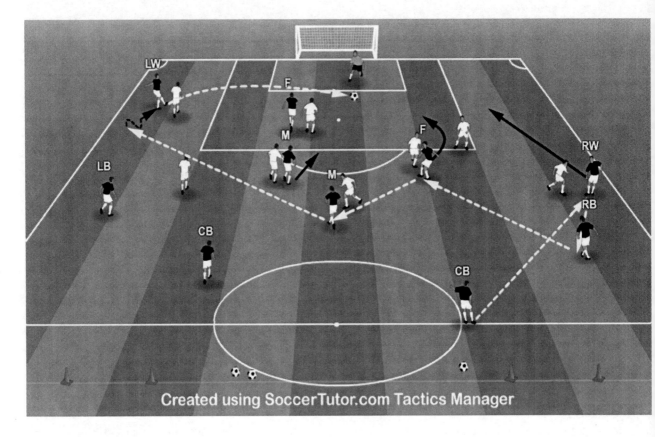

Created using SoccerTutor.com Tactics Manager

Coaching Points

1. Players must move at the right time of play, understanding all the movements of their surrounding team-mates.
2. Orientate the body, before receiving the ball, trying to get sight of the opponent's goal as quickly as possible.
3. Play quickly - one or two touches

Tactical Match - Possession and Build-Up Play

Objective

To work on possession, the tactical build up play and finishing that have beenworked on in previous practices.

Description

Play 11 v 11. If you haven't got that many players, then simply play with the numbers you have, I.e. 7 v 7 etc.

The Coach will ask during this match to try all of the combinations in the offensive half of the field stopping the game when something is being performed inaccurately or incorrectly.

Coaching Points

1. Use the exercise to practice all of the offensive exercises in previous drills by reproducing the game situation seen before.
2. Ask to develop a game with an emphasis on the possession of the ball

Session 12

15 Minutes **Two Group Technical Ball Control and Finishing Warm-Up**

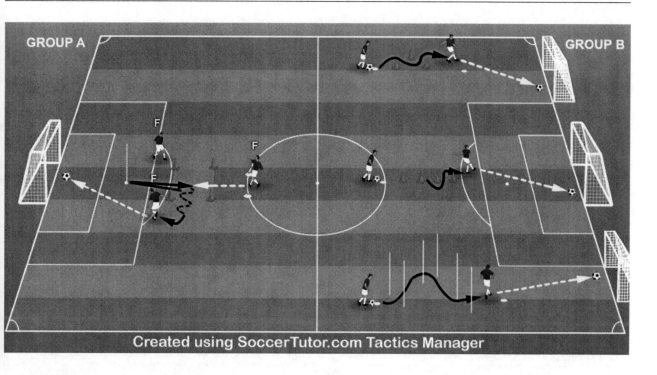

Created using SoccerTutor.com Tactics Manager

Objective
To develop ball control and finishing in warm-up practices.

Description
The team is divided into two groups:

GROUP A: (Forwards):
Forwards start in the square and must check to the yellow pole before receiving the ball with their back to the goal. The player must then quickly turn to bring the ball out of the small square with the first touch (the receiving) and shoot on goal.
- Receiving the ball with inside foot, ball on the ground and ball in the air
- Receiving the ball with outside foot, ball on the ground and ball in the air
- Receiving the ball with the chest

GROUP B: (Rest of the team):
Three stations are set-up. Players must dribble the ball in and out the cones/poles before shooting from outside the box.

Coaching Points
1. Before receiving the ball, forwards must create space - check movement.
2. Evaluate the positions of the opposition's defence before shooting on goal.
3. Positive attitude to hit the target
4. Assess what is the right position of the support foot closest to goal
5. Evaluate the chest position to avoid kicking the ball over the goal

Motor Speed 2 v 1 Exercise

15 Minutes

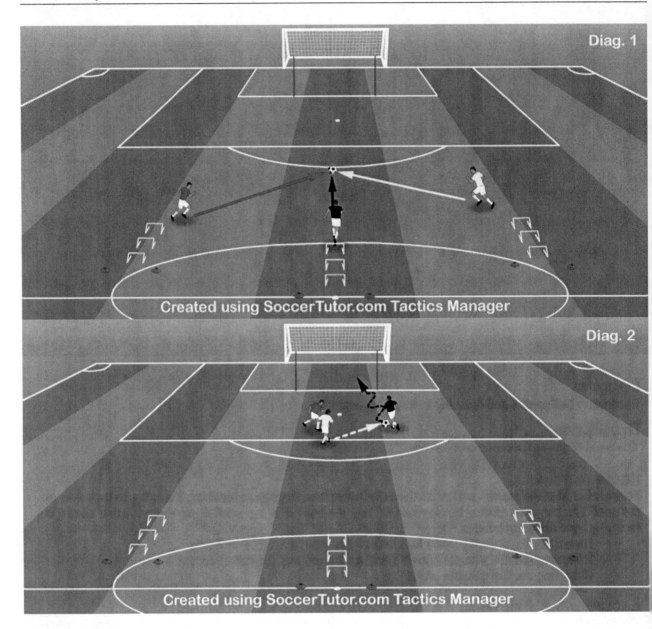

Diag. 1

Created using SoccerTutor.com Tactics Manager

Diag. 2

Created using SoccerTutor.com Tactics Manager

Objective

To develop motor speed in a fun 2 v 1 exercise.

Description

On the coach's command, three players with different colour bibs jump over the three hurdles and sprint 15 yards towards the ball.

The first player that get to the ball calls out a colour (in this case the yellow player calls out "BLUE") to play a 2 v 1 against the other colour (RED).

The objective is to score by dribbling through the goal.

Frontal 1 v 1 Situations

Created using SoccerTutor.com Tactics Manager

Objective
To develop 1 v 1 situations as well as dribbling/running with the ball and shooting.

Description
The Coach will prepare three small areas as in the diagram to avoid excessive waiting time.

1 v 1 frontal situation- If the defender recovers the ball, he will immediately shoot into one of the two small goals in front of him.

Coaching Points
1. Play fast
2. Dribble the ball with many touches
3. Try to shoot on goal immediately after feinting
4. Whilst dribbling, keep the ball near the feet
5. Try to beat the defender on his worst side

Counter-attacking from Pressing Situations

20 Minutes

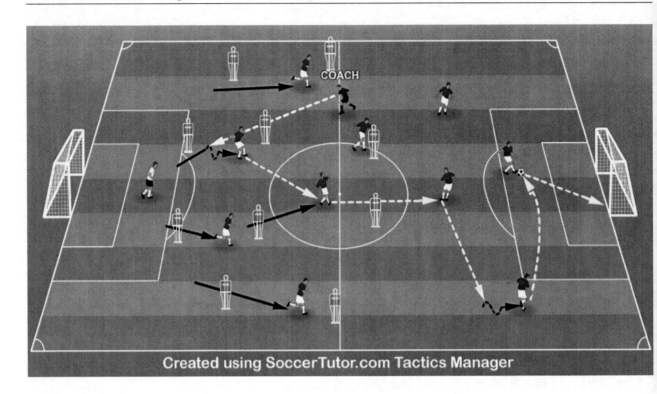

Created using SoccerTutor.com Tactics Manager

Objective

To develop counter-attacking from pressing situations.

Description

As in Session 6 - Practice 4: There are ten mannequins on the field of play (you can also use large cones) simulating the opponents. All of the mannequins are numbered 1 to10.

The coach will randomly call out a number and the team will need to move, simulating the team's need to press and cover all defensive positions, as would be the case in a real game.

To progress as shown in the above diagram: The coach will throw the ball near a mannequin, the nearest pressing player will recover it and will start the counterattack.

The team will develop different counter-attacks, trying to finish on goal within 5 passes.

Coaching Points

1. All of these actions must be performed as quickly as possible
2. Reduce the amount of touches of the ball
3. When possible, try to play using only one touch

Quick Play in a Small Sided Game Competition

Created using SoccerTutor.com Tactics Manager

Objective
To develop quick play in a small sided game competition.

Description
The team is divided into four teams of four players each (can be 3v3 or 5v5 depending on how many players you have).

Play 5 minutes for the semi-final matches. For the finals; winners of each game play each other and losers play each other, both for 10 minutes.

Coaching Points
1. Encourage players to think and play quickly, selecting the right pass before receiving the ball.
2. Correct body shape (open on the half-turn) and positioning is important in order to know where the next pass is going.

Counter-attacking Tactical Match

20 Minutes

Created using SoccerTutor.com Tactics Manager

Objective

Tactical game: using the final game to improve upon all of the counter-attacking tactical aspects.

Description

Play 11 v 11. If you haven't got that many players, then simply play with the numbers you have, I.e. 7 v 7 etc.

The Coach will stay close to the field of play with a ball in his hands. When one team will be in an offensive situation (for example with 7 players in the opponent half), he will pass the ball to the opponent's team who must develop a fast counterattack.

Coaching Points

1. Movement of players and passing must be done as quickly as possible.
2. Reduce the amount of touches on the ball to quickly get into scoring positions; ideally within five passes.

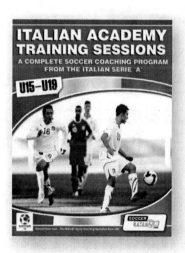

Lightning Source UK Ltd.
Milton Keynes UK
UKOW022238160413

209310UK00002B/16/P